Hanging Out
with Jesus

Hanging Out with Jesus

Bob Hartman

Illustrated by
Mark Beech

Authentic

Text copyright © Bob Hartman 2009, 2010, 2019
Illustrations copyright © Mark Beech 2009, 2010, 2019
25 24 23 22 21 20 19   7 6 5 4 3 2 1

This revised omnibus edition first published 2019 by Authentic Media
Limited,
PO Box 6326, Bletchley, Milton Keynes, MK1 9GG.
authenticmedia.co.uk

Previously published in two volumes:
Best Mates
Text copyright © Bob Hartman 2009
Illustrations copyright © Mark Beech 2009
First published 2009
Reprinted 2012

Best Mates Too!
Text copyright © Bob Hartman 2010
Illustrations copyright © Mark Beech 2010
First published 2009

British Library Cataloguing in Publication Data
A catalogue record for this book is available from the British Library.

ISBN 978-1-78893-029-1
(ISBN Best Mates 978-1-90463-754-7)
(ISBN Best Mates Too! 978-1-86024-805-4)

Printed and bound by CPI Group (UK) Ltd., Croydon, CR0 4YY

Contents

Chapter 1

WINE

"This is just the start!"

I raised my goblet of wine. "Cheers!"

"Cheers!" said my big friend, Big Bart. Then we turned to our new friend Jesus, who was standing at the other side of the room, and raised our goblets in his direction.

"Cheers!" Jesus mouthed back, and he raised his glass too.

"This 'Following Jesus' thing isn't bad," I said.

2

"Not bad at all," agreed Bart. "A little teaching. A little travelling. And now this lovely little wedding. Who did you say the bride was?"

"The oldest daughter of some friend of Jesus' mum," I shrugged. "But who cares, really. The food is good. The wine's OK. And I suppose you've noticed the bridesmaids."

"You bet!" Bart grinned. "Especially the one at the end there."

"The one with the big bunch of flowers?" I said, and then I sniggered. "Oooh, Bart has a girlfriend!"

"**SHUT UP**!" Bart grunted, and then he added sheepishly, "Do you think we can find out her name?"

"I bet Jesus' mum knows," I said. "She's right over there. **C'MON**."

So Bart and I squeezed through the crowd and crept up behind Jesus' mum.

"She's already talking to somebody," I whispered.

"She looks upset," Bart whispered back. "Maybe this isn't a good time."

"It's always a good time for LUURV!" I chuckled.

"Shut up!" Bart grunted again.

And then Jesus' mum turned around. "Can I help you?" she asked. She still didn't look very happy.

"Sorry," I said. "This is Bart and I'm Pip. We're two of your son's new . . . well, you know, his students."

"And his mates as well," added Bart.

"His disciples," Mary nodded. "Yes, I know. So perhaps you can lend me a hand, here."

"Yeah, of course," I nodded.

"Anything!" agreed Bart.

"Well," Mary sighed, "It seems they've run out of wine. Can you

believe it? A terrible embarassment for my friends! I have been trying to persuade the wedding planner here that he should do something about it, but I'm getting nowhere. So I'm going to talk to Jesus and I want you to stay here till I return. Understood?" Then she hurried off across the room, but not before saying, "Oh, and the wedding planner's name is Thomas."

"Right, then," I said to the wedding planner. "Pleased to meet you, Thomas. Nice wedding."

"And I'm sure everything will turn out fine," added Big Bart. "Beverage-wise, I mean."

"I doubt it," Thomas sighed. "I think it's more likely that the wedding will be ruined, the family will be furious, I will lose my job and then my home, and I will die in a ditch somewhere, a sad and broken man."

"Right," Bart shrugged. "Look on the BRIGHT SIDE. That's what I always say."

"But you forgot about Jesus!" I said. "Look, his mum's talking to him, now."

"He doesn't look very happy," Thomas
sighed again.

And at that point, an exasperated

"MOTHER!"

rang out across the room.

"All right, then. Maybe he won't be much help," I said. "But he's a very good teacher."

"And a great, all-round kind of guy," added Bart.

"And what's more," I whispered, "some folks even think he's the SPECIAL ONE God has promised to send us."

"The Messiah?" Thomas moaned. "I doubt it! And in any case, unless he has a wagonload of wine parked outside or a barrelful hidden beneath his robes, he's not going to be any use to me. I don't need a Messiah. I need wine!"

I looked at Bart. Bart looked at me. We both shrugged and looked at Thomas.

"Well, nice talking to you," I said.

"Yeah, UMM, all the best," mumbled Bart.

And as Thomas buried his face in his hands, we slipped away.

"That was embarrassing," Bart whispered.

"Tell me about it," I said. "What was Jesus' mum thinking? I don't have any wine. You don't have any wine. Jesus doesn't have any wine. What were we supposed to do?"

"Dunno," said Bart. "But I think we missed a chance there. I bet he knows the name of that girl."

And then someone crashed into him from behind.

"**HEY!**" Bart shouted. "Watch where you're going!" And when he whirled around, there were two servants, huffing and puffing and carrying a big stone jar between them.

"Sorry, sir," said one of the servants. "We didn't see you, and we're sort of in a hurry here."

"You don't have any wine in those jars, by any chance?" I asked.

"No, sir," the other servant apologised. "The wine is all gone. There's just water in here. That fellow over there told us to fetch it."

"And five **more** jars as well," sighed the first servant.

"That fellow over there?" asked Bart, pointing to Jesus.

"That's the one sir. And, if you'll excuse us, we've got to get on with it. These jars are kind of heavy."

Bart looked at me. And I looked at Bart.

"What do you think he's up to?" asked Bart.

"No idea," I answered. "I say we follow the men with the jars."

And so we did. And that led us straight to Jesus.

"Evening, lads," he said. "Enjoying the party?"

"Umm, absolutely," I replied. "But we were just wondering—"

"We were just wondering," Bart interrupted, seeing a chance to have two puzzles solved at once, "if you knew the name of that girl over there?"

"What girl?" asked Jesus.

"The one with the big bunch of flowers," I said.

"No, sorry," said Jesus. "I could ask my mum, though."

"Tried that," I said, glaring at Bart. "And that's what we were REALLY wondering. See, she told us about the wine."

"Ah, yes, the wine," Jesus grinned. "So she spoke to you as well, did she? Then I guess you've discovered that she can be rather . . ."

"**Persuasive?**" I suggested.

"Exactly," said Jesus. "I told her it wasn't really the time yet for this sort of thing. But, hey, she's my mum, so what could I do?"

"That's the question, isn't it?" I said. "What COULD you do – with six big jars of water?"

"Water?" chuckled Jesus, dipping a goblet into one of the jars. "No, I think if you drink this, you'll find that it's something else altogether."

14

I took a drink and Bart did too. And then
we both shouted,

Wine!

"But the servants," Bart gasped. "The servants said there was only water in them. And that was just a minute or two ago!"

"There was," Jesus shrugged. "And now there's wine. How about that!"

"But that's amazing!" I said. "That's incredible!"

"That's a MIRACLE!" cried Bart.

"A fair description," Jesus grinned. "The first, by my count, but by no means the last."

And then he put his hands on our shoulders and looked us in the eye.

"Did you lads think that this little journey of ours was only going to be about teaching and travelling and pretty girls? I told you when we began that you would see things you never,

ever imagined. And this is just the start!"

"Speaking of that," I said, "there's someone else who needs to see this – right away!" And dipping my goblet back into the jar, I hurried off to find Thomas, with Big Bart in tow.

"Here!" I said, thrusting the goblet into Thomas's hand. "Try this!"

Thomas drank the wine. And the more he drank, the BIGGER his eyes got.

"Where did you get this?" he cried.

"From the stone jars – over there," said Bart. But before he could say any more, Thomas raced over to the bridegroom.

"Sir," he said, "this last batch of wine is superb. Most hosts save the worst wine for the end of the party, when the guests are the worse for wear. But you, sir, you have saved the best for last!"

The bridegroom looked more than a little confused, but Thomas hardly noticed. He stumbled back to Bart and me, mumbling as he went, "Where was he keeping this? Why didn't he tell me? How was I supposed to know? I'll lose my job, and my house, and my dog, and—"

"It wasn't the bridegroom," I interrupted. "It was Jesus. He made the wine out of six jars of water!"

"I doubt it!" said Thomas. "That's **impossible!**"

"That's what we said," answered Bart. "But we saw it with our own eyes. And so did all your servants."

Thomas checked. He was very thorough. He asked each and every servant. And each one told him the same story.

Jesus had, indeed, changed the water into wine.

"I don't know what to think," said Thomas, shaking his head and staring at the floor.

"Somebody who could do this must be somebody very special indeed."

"Maybe even the SPECIAL ONE God promised to send us?" I suggested.

"Maybe even the MESSIAH," Thomas nodded. And then he paused. And then he turned to Bart and me. And then he asked: "I don't suppose I could come with you, could I?"

"Can't see any reason why not," said Bart. "But we'd have to check with Jesus."

"I'll do it," I offered. "I'll tell him that Thomas here wants to join us."

"It's TOMMO, actually," he said. "That's what my friends call me, anyway.

"Right, then," I nodded. "Tommo."

"Actually," said Big Bart, rubbing his hands together, "there is a little something you could do for us, in return. Do you see that girl over there?"

"The one with the big bunch of flowers?" asked Tommo.

"Yes," Bart sighed. "I just wanted to know her name, that's all."

"It's Hannah," said Tommo. "But I'm afraid to say that she's already spoken for. Do you see that guy standing next to her?"

"The one with the big muscles?" said Bart. "And the even bigger sword?"

"That's the one," nodded Tommo. "And I'm afraid that he's even bigger than you. It would take another miracle to get her away from him."

"I think you may be right, my new friend," grinned Bart. And then, like a shot, he was off.

"Where are you going?" Tommo called after him.

"Where do you think?" Bart shouted back. "I'm going to have a word with Jesus' mum. Maybe she can persuade him that it's time for MIRACLE NUMBER TWO!"

Chapter 2

ROOF

"That is, by far, the most
revolting thing I have ever smelled."

*T*he house was crowded.

Too crowded to move. Too crowded to breathe. Too crowded for the crowd that had crowded into the house – to listen to Jesus.

"Move over!" I grumbled.

"There's no room!" grunted Tommo.

"Hush!" shushed Big Bart. "Or I'll sit on both of you!"

But Jesus just looked at us and grinned. Then he finished the story he was telling, cracked a joke, and everybody laughed.

Everybody but the religious leaders, that is, who were leaning against the wall, frowning and shaking their heads and muttering.

"They're just jealous," whispered Tommo.

"'Cos they're BORING!" I said, "and Jesus isn't!"

"And if that's what you really thought," grunted Big Bart, "you'd shut up so we could hear him! REMEMBER . . ." and he said this very slowly, "Jesus is not just our friend. He's our teacher too. We're supposed to be learning something here." And he shifted his Big Bart body so that we had even less room to move.

"OK! OK!" gasped Tommo. "Point taken, Big Fella."

And I gasped as well and sniffed the air.

"All right," I muttered. "Who did it?"

"Who did what?" Tommo whispered back. And then he sniffed the air as well and gagged, "That is, by far, the most revolting thing I have ever smelt."

We both looked at Bart, who was whistling to himself and examining the ceiling.

"You know what they say," he suggested. "He who smelt it, dealt it!"

"No, he didn't!" I grunted. "That was a Big-Bart-fart if ever I smelt one!"

"If it WAS me," Bart said, "and I'm not saying it WAS, whoever did it deserves our thanks. Look, it's a lot less crowded now!"

And, sure enough, everyone around us had scooted away as far as possible.

"A job well done!" Bart grinned.

And then I gasped again.

"Definitely not me," Bart said. "One Toot at a Time. That's my rule."

"No. No, it's not that," I cried. "Up there! Look! Somebody's busting through the ceiling!"

And so somebody was. Plaster was dropping to the floor. And one, then two, then three, then four pairs of hands reached through, tearing a great big hole in the roof.

"Jesus!" shouted Bart. "Do you want me to deal with this?"

But Jesus just stared up through the hole, smiling all the while. "No, wait," he answered. "I've got a good feeling about that hole."

And as soon as he'd said it, a man came
down through the hole. A man on a mat. A mat
with a rope at each corner. A rope for each pair
of hands.

Big Bart grabbed one side. Tommo and I
grabbed the other. And when we had lowered it
gently to the floor, four heads appeared in the
hole.

"Sorry," said one head. "Our friend is sick."

"Really sorry," said another. "It was the only
way we could get him in."

"Our most sincere apologies," added a third.
"We figured Jesus could make him well."

"And . . . UMM . . . well . . . that's about all
there is to say," muttered the fourth head.
"Sorry. Won't happen again."

"Seems reasonable," I whispered.

"It's not YOUR house," grunted Tommo.

"That roof really tied the room together,"
sighed Big Bart. Then he nudged us so hard he

nearly knocked us over, and whispered. "Here it comes. Jesus is going to do something amazing again!"

But Jesus didn't do that. He didn't do anything at first. He looked at the man. He looked at us. He looked at the religious leaders. He had a look in his eye that looked like he was up to SOMETHING. And when at last he spoke, what he said was:

"My friend, your sins are forgiven."

"Didn't see that coming," whispered Bart.

"Me neither," nodded Tommo.

"Won't help much, come the next Fun Run," I noted. "But it's still a nice thing for him to do."

The religious leaders, however, were furious.

"Look at their faces!" I said.

"I've never seen them so angry!" said Tommo.

"I think that's steam coming out of their ears," noted Bart.

Huffing and puffing and sputtering with rage,

 one of the religious leaders shook his fist and shouted,

"Who do you think you are? Only God can forgive sin!"

Jesus winked at us.

"All right, then," he answered,

"here's a question for you. Which is easier – to forgive a man's sins or to make him walk?"

Big Bart slowly raised his hand.

And Tommo slowly pulled it down again.

"Jesus doesn't want an answer," he whispered. "He's trying to make a point!"

"But I know the answer!" Bart whispered back. "They're both impossible – and only somebody amazing could do either of them."

So that's what Jesus did. Something AMAZING.

"To show you that I have both the power and the right to fix what is wrong in this man's heart," said Jesus, "I will fix what is wrong with his legs."

Then he looked at the man and said, "Get up, my friend. **Get up and walk**."

And so the man did. And with his friends cheering from above and the crowd cheering below, he picked up his mat and walked out of the house!

Everyone followed, even the religious leaders, still muttering amongst themselves.

Most of Jesus' disciples went, too, leaving Tommo and Bart and me to bring up the rear.

"So where are you three going?" asked Jesus.

"With the others," I answered.

"To join the celebration," said Tommo.

"IT'S PARTY TIME!" boomed Big Bart.

Jesus looked at the three of us and then he looked at the ceiling. He looked like he was up to something again.

"You're my friends, right?" he asked.

And each of us nodded.

"But you want to learn something from me as well, don't you?"

We nodded again.

"Well, lads, I grew up in the home of a carpenter . . ."

I looked up at the hole.

"I knew that," I said.

Tommo looked up, too, and groaned.

"I see where this is going."

Big Bart's gaze followed ours.

"I don't get it," he said. And then he sighed, "Oh, yes I do."

"That's right," grinned Jesus. "It's time to show you three how to fix a roof!"

Then he sniffed the air, wrinkled his nose, and asked, "Did one of you just . . .?"

I looked at Bart.

Tommo did too.

"One TOOT at a Time," Bart shrugged. And then we noticed the man. The man with the mat. The man who couldn't walk. The man who was walking now.

"Looks like his legs aren't the only things that are working again," Jesus chuckled.

Then he hurried away, up the stairs to the roof – with the three of us close behind.

Chapter 3

SABBATH

"Bart, you still have
barley up your nose."

*I*t was the Sabbath.

We were walking with Jesus and the rest of his disciples – wandering through a field of barley.

And, as often happened, Tommo and Big Bart and I had fallen a little way behind.

"I'm hungry!" moaned Bart.

"You're always hungry!" groaned Tommo.

"But I'm hungry too," I moaned. "So hungry I could eat a camel."

"I could eat a camel and its mum," sighed Bart. "All covered in rich camelly sauce."

"With a cherry on top!" I added.

"Shut up both of you!" grunted Tommo. "Everybody's hungry – all right? But there's no camels or camels' mums or camelly sauce around. There's just barley. Acres and acres of barley!"

"I could eat some barley," I said.

"I could eat some barley and its mum," added Bart.

"Barley doesn't have a mum," muttered Tommo.

"That's so sad!" I sighed. "No mum. No dad. Just little bitty baby barleys!"

"With a cherry on the top!" Bart chuckled.

Tommo shook his head and sighed. Then he snapped off a bit of barley and tossed it to me.

"Just shut up and eat."

"WHOA!" said Bart. "Tommo just borrowed some barley!"

"I think, 'Stole' is the preferred word," I added.

"It's called 'gleaning'," Tommo sighed.

"Stealing. Gleaning. I don't care what you call it," said Bart. "You just swiped somebody's barley!"

Tommo sighed. "It's **not** stealing, it's gleaning. And it's perfectly legal. Look, I was raised on a farm. Where do you two come from?"

"Seaside," I replied.

"Well, if you go down that road till you come to the hill that looks like the High Priest's bottom . . ." Bart began.

Tommo glared.

"Town," Bart muttered. "I come from a town."

"Then, listen and learn," Tommo grunted. "My father was a farmer and it was his duty to leave a little of his crop behind so that passing strangers and the poor would have something to eat. That's called **gleaning**, and that's all that we're doing. Got it?" And he tossed some barley to Bart too.

"I got it," said Bart. "But I don't know what to do with it."

"Roll it round in your hands," explained Tommo, "and the bits of grain will come off and you can pop them into your mouth."

"Or you can toss them in the air and catch them," I said.

"That looks like fun!" Bart replied. And he tried it as well. He tossed one bit of

grain and caught it. He tossed two. But when the third bit came down, he shook his head and muttered, "DUH-OH."

"What now?" groaned Tommo.

"Id wed ub by dose," said Bart.

"For heaven's Sake!" Tommo groaned again. "How did it get up your nose?"

"I tossed id in da air and breadthed ad da sabe tibe," Bart shrugged. "And id wed ub by dose."

"Just blow it out!" I said.

"I'll dry," said Bart. But before he blew out, he sniffed in, and "DUH-OH."

"You snorted it further in!" I cried.

"Do. Well, yes. But I said 'DUH-OH' because we're dod alode. Look!"

Tommo and I turned around – and jumped. There were two religious leaders standing behind us, arms folded and faces red.

"And what do you think you're doing?" they scowled.

"Dot stealing," said Bart. "Hodest."

"We're just gleaning," said Tommo, "and as I explained to my friends, here, it's perfectly legal."

"Not on the Sabbath day!" shouted one of the religious leaders.

"The Sabbath," Tommo sighed.

"Hadn't thought of that," I added.

And Big Bart just said, "DUH-OH," again.

"Indeed!" shouted the other religious leader. "No one is allowed to work on the Sabbath day.

And, strictly speaking, gleaning and eating the gleanings is work."

Bart raised his hand. "Stricdly speakig, nod all ob us were eatig. Sub ob us were just sdiffing. See, I god sub ub by dose."

"IT DOESN'T MATTER!" they both shouted. "You were working! That is against the rules of our religion! And you, followers of Rabbi Jesus!"

"Don't bring Jesus into this!" I said. "He's our friend."

"And your teacher!" sneered one of the religious leaders.

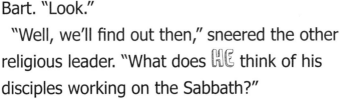

"And he's cubbing here right dow," said Bart. "Look."

"Well, we'll find out then," sneered the other religious leader. "What does HE think of his disciples working on the Sabbath?"

"Greetings, lads," said Jesus.

Then he nodded in the direction of the religious leaders, "Gentlemen."

And finally he smiled and said, "Barley. Excellent. I'm **starving!**" And he tore a bit off, rubbed it between his hands, and went to pop it in his mouth.

"Do, Jesus, don't!" Bart cried. "Dese ben bill dink you are bad!"

Jesus paused. "What did he say?"

I scratched my head and said, "I think it was something like, 'No, Jesus, don't. These men will think you are bad.'"

Bart nodded enthusiastically, and Jesus said, "That's what I thought. The problem is that these men already think I'm bad. Because I

50

don't talk about God the same way they do.
And because I think that people's needs are
more important than their rules."

Then he popped a bit of barley into his mouth,
and the religious
leaders went mad!

"SEE!" shrieked
one of them,
"Jesus is doing
it too!"

"He's breaking
the Sabbath
rules!" shrieked
the other.

"Calm down," Jesus said. "And let me ask you a question. You remember King David, don't you?"

"Of **course** we do!" they grunted. "He was the greatest king our people ever had!"

"Yes, he was," Jesus nodded. "A man after God's own heart. That's what our sacred book says."

"**EXACTLY**," the leaders grunted again. **"So?"**

"So," Jesus continued, "when David and his followers were hungry once, they went to a holy place and they ate the special holy bread that the rules said should only be eaten by the priests."

"I did not know that," whispered Tommo.

"I'd hate to hab a loaf ob sbecial holy bread up by dose," whispered Bart.

"And the point is . . .?" sneered the religious leaders.

"The point," Jesus grinned, "is that David broke the religious rules to meet the needs of his friends. And that is all that WE are doing."

"But you're NOT King David!" they answered.

"No," said Jesus. "But I AM The Son of Man! And the Son of Man gets to say what happens on the Sabbath."

And at that, the religious leaders grew more furious still.

"The Son of Man?" I whispered.

"The Messiah!" Tommo whispered back. "The Son of Man is another name for the Messiah —

the Special One God has always promised to
send us!"

"I still hab sub barley ub by dose," Bart
reminded us.

"Ridiculous!" shouted one of the religious
leaders.

"PREPOSTEROUS! OUTRAGEOUS!"

shouted the other. "We intend to report this incident to the highest authorities. We're not finished with you, Jesus!"

And they stomped away across the field, even angrier than when they had arrived.

Tommo looked at Jesus, slack-jawed, open-mouthed.

"So you're saying . . . I mean, you really are . . .?"

"I'm saying that it's time to go," Jesus smiled. "And perhaps I'll say more later. But for now, we'd better catch up with the others. And, yes Bart, I know, you still have barley up your nose. Why don't you just blow it out?"

"Tried that, Jesus," I said. "But all he did was—" And Bart made the most awful noise. "See?"

"No, Bart," Jesus sighed. "That's snorting."

"How aboud dis den?" Bart said. And he made another noise.

"No, Bart," Jesus sighed again. "That's hawking."

"But look!" Bart grinned, holding out his hand. "There it is!"

"So it is, Bart," Jesus sighed a third time. "And that – that is disgusting!"

"So there are some things even you think shouldn't happen on the Sabbath, eh Jesus?" I chuckled.

"Or any other day of the week," muttered Jesus. "Now let's get going."

And so we went, across the fields of barley and off to join our other friends.

Chapter 4

FUNERAL

"Poke the badger
and see what's inside!"

*T*ommo, Big Bart and I were walking along the dusty Galilean road. But we weren't alone. Not by a long shot.

"Kinda crowded today," I said.

"I don't know half these people," added Bart.

"Well, they're just doing what we're doing," grinned Tommo. "Following after Jesus."

"I reckon it's the miracles," I said.

"I reckon it's what he says," Bart shrugged. "The way he stands up to those stuffy religious leaders."

Tommo leaned over and whispered, like he was passing on a secret. "I reckon it's because they think that You-Know-Who is the You-Know-What."

"No, who? No, what?" Bart whispered back.

Tommo rolled his eyes. "Jesus. The Messiah. The Special One God promised to send us. To save us from our enemies."

"Well, whatever it is," I said, "Jesus is turning out to be one popular guy. And we are his popular friends!"

"His ENTOURAGE," said Tommo.

"His PERSONAL POSSE," chuckled Bart, "who can't wait to see what happens next."

And then, suddenly, he jumped, and he yelled, and he shielded his eyes from the side of the road.

"**What's up**, Big Fella?" I asked.

"Dead thing. Dead thing," Bart whimpered. "Decayed. Decomposing. Down in that gulch, see?"

"Yeah, I see it." Tommo shrugged. "Dead donkey. So?"

"So I hate dead animals!" Bart SHuddered.
"Hate to look at them. Hate to smell them.
Hate to be anywhere near them!"

"**yeah**," I sighed. "Kind of reminds you of
your own demise, doesn't it? One day we'll all
be there. Dead as donkeys. Flies buzzing up our
noses. Vultures pecking out our eyes . . ."

"SHUT UP! SHUT UP!" Bart cried.
And he stuck his fingers in his ears. Which
meant he could see the dead donkey again. So
he shut his eyes too.

"You're going to trip," I warned him, pulling
one finger from one ear. "And roll down the hill.
And end up like that donkey."

"If it's any help," added Tommo, pulling the other finger out of the other ear, "when the Messiah comes, he's going to make sure that we all go to God's Big Banquet when we die – that we all come back to life again! So if **You-Know-Who** is the **You-Know-What** . . ."

"No, who? No, what?" asked Bart.

65

"JESUS! THE MESSIAH!" Tommo sighed. "If he's the One, then we won't have to worry about being dead as donkeys!"

"But that's not what I'm worried about!" Bart sighed back.

"What is it, then, Big Fella?" I joked. "Some deep, disturbing childhood memory?"

Bart nodded, put his arms around us, and pulled us close. "Very disturbing." He shuddered. "**Very disturbing** indeed!

"I was just a kid. Five, maybe six, years old. Dead animals didn't bother me then. I'd rip the legs off dead insects, the wings off dead birds, the tails off dead rodents . . ."

"We get the picture, Bart," said Tommo. "You were a baby barbarian."

Bart chuckled. "Funny. My gran used to call me that. Anyway, one day my older brothers came running up to me. They'd found a dead rock badger on the road just outside of town. It was all bloated up, like a puffy brown ball, just stewing there in the noonday sun.

"'BIG BARTY!' they dared me (I was always tall for my age). 'Here's a stick. Poke the badger and see what's inside!'

"Now maybe they knew what would happen and maybe they didn't. But I didn't need much coaxing. I'd never looked inside a rock badger before and I was curious to find out what was in there.

"I bent over the badger, eyes and mouth both wide open. I bent over close, expecting to find a pile of guts and goo. But when I stuck the stick into that bloated body, what came out instead, was the most horrible smell I have

ever smelt – and thousands and thousands of flies! The smell went up my nose and my mouth. And the flies followed! I gagged and I choked and I . . . are you two all right?"

Tommo turned a pale shade of green.

I gulped back something. "We get the point," I said. "As you say, disturbing."

And then a cry came from somewhere at the front of the crowd. A piercing cry.

"That's pretty disturbing too," said Tommo. "I wonder what's up?"

We pushed our way to the front of the crowd. And what we found, when we got there, was another crowd coming the other way. And a lot more of those disturbing cries.

"It's a funeral procession," said Tommo.

And I put my hands over Big Bart's eyes.

"It'll be all right, Big Fella," I said. "We're here for you."

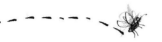

But Bart just pushed them away.

"I'm fine." He shrugged. "It's dead animals I don't like. I don't mind dead people."

I sighed. "You are an unusual human being, my friend. Has anyone ever told you that?"

And Bart started counting on his fingers.

"Well, there was my gran, of course. And that very short man who lived at the end of our street. And my Aunt Mabel – she was a professional mourner, you know, like the ones crying up there."

"Really?" I said, covering my ears. "Was she as loud as this bunch?"

"**MUCH LOUDER**!" Bart shouted. "She even won a competition, once."

"For mourning?" I asked.

"No, for making pies," said Bart. "'Bartholomew,' she used to tell me, 'the louder we cry, the louder the grieving family can cry. And it's a good thing to cry when someone dies.'

"She was a wise woman, my Aunt Mabel, with a face like a bat. Small children were terrified of her."

"Right," said Tommo. "I think we've heard **enough** stories about your family for one day. Let's see if we can shift this crowd and let the funeral pass."

"**Jesus!**" he said. "What do you want us to do?"

"Tell the folks who are following me to squeeze over to one side," said Jesus. And then he stopped and then he stared, like he'd seen a ghost.

"Everything OK, Jesus?" asked Bart.

"I know her," whispered Jesus. "The woman by the funeral bier." And he wiped something from his eye.

The weeping and the wailing went on, but for Jesus, it was suddenly like there was no one else around.

"I grew up not far from here," Jesus explained. "And that woman's husband used to come to my dad's carpenter shop. He made tools."

"SEE!" Bart whispered to Tommo. "Jesus has family stories too!"

"SHUT UP!" Tommo whispered back. "At least his family was normal."

Bart shook his head. "Who knows? As my wise, bat-faced aunt used to say, 'Every family has its secrets!'"

"They had a son," Jesus went on. "He was maybe ten years younger than me. I used to watch him sometimes, when his dad was working. Play ball with him, that sort of thing. But the father died. I remember hearing that. And the son, the son was left to take care of the mum, and, now, oh, please God, No!"

And Jesus walked over and looked at the bier. And saw the dead son. And said to the woman, "Don't cry."

"Can't see my aunt agreeing with that," Bart whispered. "'You can never get enough,' she'd say."

"What? Of crying?" I whispered.

"No, pies," said Bart.

"Can't you two shut up for even a minute?" grunted Tommo. "Look. Jesus is laying his hand on the funeral bier."

I looked around. "He can't do that. That's against the religious laws. It will make him unclean!"

"WELL, HE'S DOING IT!" said Bart. "And he's saying something too."

Everyone was listening now. The weeping and the wailing had stopped and everyone was looking at Jesus, waiting to see what the man who had stopped a funeral would do.

So Jesus did something.

He **leaned** over the corpse and he said, "Time to get up, my friend."

And then the young man did something too.

He got up. And he looked at Jesus. And he smiled and he said, "Nap time. That's what you used to say at the end of nap time. And then we'd go play ball."

"Then your dad would take you home to your mum," Jesus grinned. "I remember. There she is now."

And the young man's mum embraced him, and Jesus too, and a roar rang out from the crowd.

"A great prophet is among us! God has come to help his people."

"What did I tell you?" said Tommo. "They think that **You-Know-Who** is the **You-Know-What**."

"No, who? No, what?" asked Bart.

"**JESUS! THE MESSIAH!**" said Tommo. "He's raising people from the dead, now! How amazing is that?"

"Pretty amazing!" I grinned.

"Waste of a perfectly good funeral, though." Bart shrugged. "I mean, they'll still have to pay the caterers and the bearers and the mourners. As my aunt used to say—"

"We don't CARE what your aunt used to say!" shouted Tommo.

"The boy was dead!" I said.

"And now he's alive!" said Tommo. "And that means—"

Bart held his finger in the air. "That **You-Know-Who** is the **You-Know-What**!"

"EXACTLY!" beamed Tommo.

"And that one day we will be raised from the dead as well!" Bart continued.

"There you go, Big Fella," I beamed.

"And there will be no more dead people or dead donkeys or dead rock badgers," Bart went on.

"That's it!" cheered Tommo.

"And we will sit at God's Big Forever Banqueting Table . . . and . . . and . . ."

"**yes**?" said Tommo.

"GO ON!" I said.

Bart thought for a moment, then a big, bat-like grin spread across his Big Bart face.

"And eat PIES!"

Chapter 5

SOLDIER

"If you follow me,
you're going to be surprised."

*T*ommo, Big Bart and I were shuffling along the sandy seashore. Shuffling along behind Jesus and his other friends.

The sun was bright. The breeze was warm. The day was perfect!

"Ah, the sea," sighed Tommo.

"Ah, Capernaum," sighed Big Bart.

"Ah, Capernaum-by-the-Sea," I sighed, too.

"That's what my cousin Sam calls it. And he has plans for this place."

"Do tell," said Tommo, sitting himself down on the sand.

"We're all ears," added Big Bart, settling down beside him.

"It's like this," I began, squeezing between the two. "Sam reckons that, one day, we won't have to spend all our time working – so we will go away to 'Special' places."

"Like the Temple?" said Tommo. "For fasts and festivals? We do that now."

"That's not exactly what he means—" I said.

"Oh, I know," interrupted Bart, thrusting his hand into the air. "It's like when we go to visit my gramma Huldah. She makes amazing bread.

And cakes. And she has a wart on her nose that looks like the High Priest."

"No. No," I insisted. "It's neither of those. It's not religious. It's not a family visit. It's a special kind of place where people will go to have fun."

"**Fun?**" asked Tommo and Bart together. "In Capernaum?"

"Capernaum-by-the-Sea!" I grinned. And then I started pointing. "Sam wants to build some little huts over there, where people will play games and win things. He wants to fence off another area for donkey rides. And he's come up with this incredible recipe for really chewy honey cakes. They're built up in layers and when you bite into them, you find 'Capernaum' written inside!"

Tommo rolled his eyes. "You know what I think? I think that if you bit into your cousin, you'd find 'GOOFY' written inside."

"Yeah," nodded Bart. Nobody is ever going to go to the seaside to have fun! It's too cold and windy."

"And there's sand EVERYWHERE!" added Tommo.

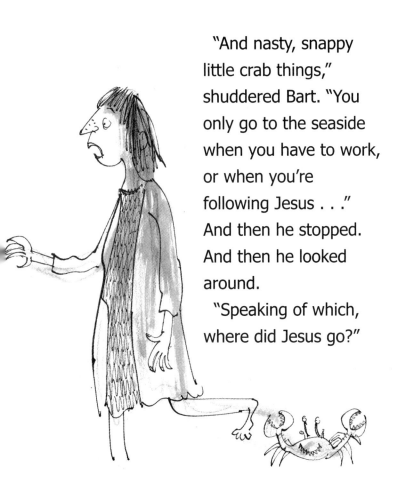

"And nasty, snappy little crab things," shuddered Bart. "You only go to the seaside when you have to work, or when you're following Jesus . . ." And then he stopped. And then he looked around.

"Speaking of which, where did Jesus go?"

Tommo and I looked as well. Jesus was out of sight.

"He can't be far," I said, jumping to my feet and brushing the sand from my bottom.

"I bet he's gone up the High Street," suggested Bart. "If we hurry we can catch him."

"Too bad we don't have one of your cousin's donkeys to ride on!" sniggered Tommo.

So, kicking sand, then pebbles, then dirt, we raced from the beach to the High Street.

"THERE HE IS!" said Tommo.

"He hasn't gone far,"
I added.

And then Big Bart
stretched out his two big
arms and grabbed us
both.

"That's because he had
to stop. Look, there's a
Roman soldier coming
down the street, headed
right for him."

"And it's not just any
soldier," added Tommo.
"Do you see the helmet
and the standard? It's
a centurion!"

"Should we run?" I whispered.

"Run?" Bart growled. "That's the last thing I want to do. If I had my way . . . I'd . . . I'd . . ." And he slammed his big fist into his big hand.

"Steady, Big Fella," cautioned Tommo. "They've got spears and swords and all sorts."

"I **hate** 'em," Bart growled again. "And that's all there is to it. Especially the centurions. My grampa Abe was in the market one day, just minding his own business, when this centurion ordered one of his men to grab him and load two sackfuls of grain onto his back. He had a **hundred** soldiers under him, for heaven's sake, all of them fit and strong, and he had to pick on an old man."

Tommo shook his head. "WOW. I didn't know. Sorry."

"And that's why I ask again," I asked again, "should we run?"

"We're supposed to be following Jesus," said Tommo. "How do you think he'd feel if we chickened out on him now?"

"**Dunno**," I shrugged. "I just find that avoiding Roman soldiers is a lot better than dealing with them. And making jokes – that helps."

"Jokes?" grunted Bart.

"Yes," I smiled weakly. "Here's one: what's the difference between an onion and a Roman centurion?"

They just stared at me, arms crossed.

"C'MON," I said.

"All right," sighed Tommo. "What's the difference between an onion and a Roman centurion?"

"People cry when they chop up an onion!" I grinned. "Here's another one: a man walks into a bar with a lion. 'Do you serve Roman centurions here?' he asks. '**Certainly do!**' says the waiter. '**Fine**,' says the man. 'I'll have a beer, and my lion will have the centurion!'"

Bart let out a small chuckle.

"You liked that one, didn't you, Big Fella?" I chuckled back. "My motto is: 'If you can't beat 'em, make fun of 'em.'"

"Well," said Tommo. "My motto is: 'When the Messiah comes, he'll chuck them all out and our people will be free again!' And if Jesus is who I think he is, then that

centurion who stopped him is about to take on more than he can handle. C'mon."

So with Tommo leading the way, we walked up the street, until we were standing behind Jesus, with the rest of his friends.

The centurion spoke first. "Lord," he said to Jesus, "I have a servant. He's ill. He's lying at home in terrible pain."

"Did you hear that?" Tommo whispered. "He called Jesus 'Lord'! He recognises that Jesus is somebody special."

"Somebody who is about to deliver a special put-down," grunted Bart.

"Hey, I thought of another one," I said. "How do you save a Roman soldier from drowning?"

But before I could deliver my punchline, Jesus answered the centurion.

"Take me to your servant," he said. "I'd be happy to make him well."

"**What**?" growled Bart.

"I did not expect that!" whispered Tommo.

"Take your foot off his throat," I chuckled. "Get it? He's only drowning in the first place cause his head is underwater and you've . . . got . . . your . . . foot . . . Did I miss something?"

"Jesus is going to help him!" Bart gasped. "A Roman! A CENTURION!"

"I don't get it!" Tommo gasped back. "If Jesus is the Messiah, then he's supposed to help us, God's special people. Not our enemies!"

The centurion bowed his head.

"Lord," he said again. "I know what I am. I know what my job is. I know what you and your people must think of me. And therefore I know that I do not deserve to have you come to my house."

"He can say that again," whispered Tommo. And Jesus turned around and "shushed" him.

"But because I am a soldier," the centurion continued, "I also know something about giving orders. When I tell my men to do something, they do it. No questions asked. I see that same kind of power, that same kind of authority, in you. So give the order, tell the sickness to go away, and I am confident that my servant will be healed."

Jesus just stood there for a second, staring at the centurion. We had seen Jesus do some shocking things, but we had never seen **him** shocked. And when at last he opened his mouth, all Jesus could say was, "**WOW**!"

Then he turned to all of us. "Did you hear that?" he said. "This man trusts me. He really does."

Then he looked right at me and Tommo and Big Bart.

"I know that some of you hate him and fear him and all he stands for. And you may well have good reason. But I have yet to find among our own people anyone who trusts me like this.

"I just want you to know that, if you follow me, you're going to be **SURPRISED**. People from all across this world – not just our friends, but our enemies too – will one day find their way to the big banquet God has waiting for us at the end of time.

"He doesn't look at the badges on helmets or the colour of faces or races. He looks at the heart. He looks for those who trust him."

Then Jesus turned back to the centurion and said,

"**GO HOME**. Your servant is already well."

And the three of us watched him go, then looked down at our feet and shuffled our sandals.

"Guess we were supposed to learn something there," muttered Bart.

"Not sure I like it much," Tommo muttered back.

"I have another joke," I said weakly.

"GIVE IT A BREAK!" sighed the other two.

"No, I want to hear it," said Jesus, who had wandered up behind us. "I like a good joke."

"You're not going to like this one, Jesus," said Tommo.

"**Trust us**," added Big Bart.

"Go on, Pip," said Jesus. "I'm all ears."

"Well," I said, thinking as quickly as I could. "What do you call a nice Roman who trusts Jesus and who just had his servant healed, while he is riding in his chariot?"

"Don't know," said Jesus. "What do you call a nice Roman who trusts Jesus and who just had his servant healed, while he is riding in his chariot?"

"A HOLY ROLLER!" I chuckled.

Bart, Tommo and Jesus looked at each other.

They looked at the ground. A cricket chirped somewhere in the distance.

"Right then," said Jesus. "I'm off. Anybody following?"

"That'll be me," said Tommo.

"Right behind you," added Bart.

"Don't you get it?" I pleaded. "He's holy. He's rolling. He's . . . I don't know. But it sounds funny. Maybe you'll get it . . . maybe I'll get it . . . someday. Hey, wait for me!"

And I ran off after my friends.

In the general direction of the sea.

Chapter 6

STORM

'Save a seat in your
heavenly whale for me!'

Big Bart crossed his arms and stood stock still, like an enormous statue.

"I'm not going," he grunted. "Don't ask me again."

"But the boat is ready to go!" I sighed. "Everyone's waiting."

"Don't care," muttered Bart. "Not going."

"Chicken," clucked Tommo.

"Not going."

"Cluck-cluck-cluck!" I added.

"Sticks and stones," Bart answered.

"Not going. NOT going. NOT GOING!"

"But everybody else is going!" I pleaded.

Bart recrossed his arms and sighed.

"To quote my dear old mum: 'If everybody else jumped off a very high tower or a very high mountain or some other very high thing, would that make it all right for you to jump off as well?'" And then, without waiting for a reply, he added, "Thought not."

"But **nobody's** jumping off a very high thing," argued Tommo. "Jesus just wants us to get in the boat and cross the lake. He's our teacher. He's our friend. Is it so much to ask?"

"So much to ask?" asked Big Bart. "Why don't you ask my great-uncle Jonah? Oh, that's right. **YOU CAN'T!** And why can't you? Because my great-uncle Jonah is dead! That's right – dead, DEPARTED, DECEASED!"

I rolled my eyes. "We've heard the story before. There's no need—"

"Oh, I think there's need!" Bart interrupted. "A great big stinking pile of need! You may have listened to the story, but as our friend Jesus is always telling us, you did not have 'ears to hear' the warning within!"

And then he uncrossed his arms and held them wide in a dramatic pose.

"I was just a tiddler, and there we were, at the annual Sea of Galilee Water Jubilee. It was the tenth anniversary, and the organisers decided to put on a pageant to celebrate the date. The story of Jonah was chosen, because of its nautical theme, and my great-uncle was asked to play the lead role. An obvious choice—"

"Because of his name . . ." Tommo interrupted.

Big Bart glared. "Because of his stage presence and **booming** voice!" Bart boomed. "Half the men in my village are called Jonah, but only my uncle could have played that part.

"There was, however, **one small problem**. Like me, Great-Uncle Jonah was no fan of the high seas. So his friends – his so-called friends – persuaded him to take the role.

"All went well, at first. A local fishing boat served as the ship-set-sail-for-Tarshish. But when Uncle Jonah was tossed from that ship into the mouth of a great floating wooden whale, built specially for the occasion, the force of his landing made it leak and the whale began to sink! Poor Uncle Jonah's foot was trapped between two wooden whale molars, and like his namesake, he was carried by the whale to the bottom of this very lake."

Tommo glanced at me and shook his head. He was trying very hard not to laugh.

"Well, we're sorry your great-uncle died in the mouth of a giant fake whale . . ."

"Oh, he didn't die," said Bart. "He was rescued and passed away quietly in his bed, ten years later." And then his voice fell to a whisper. "But the horror, the horror of that moment never left him."

Just then, Jesus walked by.

"So are you coming?" he asked, and he smiled especially hard at Bart. "The trip will be just fine."

"ABSOLUTELY!" I answered.

"Just say the word," added Tommo.

"Ready when you are!" said Bart, with a little wave.

Jesus hopped into the boat, and Tommo and I just stared at Bart.

"So what happened to 'NOT GOING'?" asked Tommo.

"And the memory of your dear departed uncle?" I added.

"I don't know," Bart shrugged. "That 'follow me' look in his eye – it gets me every time." Then he leapt on board, with Tommo and me close behind.

Everything went well at first, but the further we sailed from the shore, the choppier the waves became. And the greener Bart's face grew!

"Not looking good, Big Fella," said Tommo.

"Maybe you'd better lie down," I suggested.

Bart waved us away and opened his mouth as though to say, "I'll be fine," or "It'll pass," or "Don't worry," but what came out instead was "Hwork!" and the better part of his breakfast.

Tommo peeped overboard. "Toast. Eggs. Porridge. You ate well, my friend."

But all Bart could do was "Hwork!" again.

"Looks like lunch, this time," I observed. "The bread and meat I recognise, but what are all those tiny yellow things?"

Jesus was looking now too. "Corn," he noted, matter-of-factly. "A bit of a minor miracle, I'd

say, seeing as we won't see corn in this part of the world for another fourteen hundred years or so."

"How about that!" said Tommo.

"Well done, Big Fella!" I added.

But all Bart could offer was another "Hwork!"

It wasn't long, however, before everyone on board was looking for a different kind of miracle. Choppy waves turned to churning waves and then to stormy waves that washed right over the boat.

"HELP!" cried Tommo.

"SAVE US!" I cried.

"I'M COMING, UNCLE JONAH!" cried Big Bart. "Save a seat in your heavenly whale for me!"

We weren't the only ones crying for help. Peter and Andrew and the rest of the fishermen were terrified too. And Jesus?

"Where's Jesus?" called Tommo. "He was here a minute ago."

"Can't see him!" I called back. "I hope he wasn't washed out to sea!"

And then, over the roaring of the storm, we heard somebody . . . Snoring.

"FOUND HIM!" hollered Big Bart. "And you'll never guess. He's asleep!"

"Wake up, Jesus! WAKE UP!" we all cried together.

And Jesus opened his eyes. And rubbed his eyes. And sat up slowly. And shook his head. Did I miss anything?"

"Miss anything?" shouted Tommo. "Look!"

And, just then, an enormous wave knocked us all off our feet. "Point taken," said Jesus. And he looked up at the thundery sky and said quietly, "Lighten up. It's getting a little noisy down here."

Then he turned to the churning waves and added, "You need to calm down too." And not a second later, the sea was still, the sun was shining, and the sky was a bright, light blue!

Jesus looked at Bart and smiled. "Told you the trip would be fine." Then he curled up again and fell back to sleep.

Bart shook his big head. He could hardly believe it.

"Now that's what I call a miracle, lads!"
he said. But Tommo and I weren't listening.

The storm had churned our stomachs up
along with the waves, and we were hanging
over the side of the boat.

"Look," said Bart. "More yellow things! Now
you're making those little miracles too!"

Chapter 7

PIGS

"I think I need my mum!"

Big Bart fell out of the boat and kissed the ground.

"Dry land at last!" he cried.

"Don't know what your problem is," Tommo shrugged.

"Yeah, Jesus made the storm go away," I said. "What more do you want? C'mon. Speak up."

"Thorry," spat Big Bart. "Thand in my mouth. Nathty. But at leathst we're thafe."

"Wouldn't speak so fast, Big Fella," sighed Tommo. "Look."

Bart lifted his face from the beach. He was looking straight at a graveyard.

"This 'following Jesus' thing certainly has its ups and downs," I noted.

"Mothtly downth at the moment," said Bart, spitting out the last bit of sand and climbing to his feet.

"Well, we could always go back on board," grinned Tommo.

"Pigs will fly before I get back on that boat," grunted Bart.

And then someone, or something, let out a blood-curdling Scream that sounded a bit like a pig. A pig in pain. Lots of pigs in pain. And I leapt up into Big Bart's arms.

"Who's the chicken, now?" chuckled Bart.

But Jesus looked serious. Very serious, indeed.

"TROUBLE," he said. "I'm going off to have a look. Tommo, make sure everyone stays together."

So off Jesus went, among the tombs, while Tommo made sure that everyone was present and accounted for.

"All right, lads," he announced. "Let's form an orderly queue. Thank you. Let's see now . . .

Peter, Andrew,
James, John . . ."
And he worked his
way right down to,
"Bartholomew,
Pip (happy to
see you
back on your
own feet!) and . . .
and . . . sorry, I
don't seem to
know your name,"
he said to the last
man in the line.

And that's when the man let out another blood-curdling scream.

And both Tommo and I leapt into Big Bart's arms.

"He's SCARY!" I cried.

"He's got chains dangling from his arms!" cried Tommo.

"And he's NAKED!" cried Bart. "Icch."

"He's got a demon inside him!" cried Jesus, racing to our rescue. And he called to the demon, "What's your name?"

"Legion!" many voices squealed back.

"Correction," said Jesus. "A whole mess of demons!"

Then the demons screamed again. "Jesus, Son of God, what do you want with us?"

"I want to go home," whimpered Bart. "I think I need my mum!"

Jesus shook his head. "No. There's a man in there too. A man like one of us. And, scary as this is, we need to stay here and help him."

Then he turned to the demons and said, "I want you to come out of this man. And I want you to do it NOW!"

The demons screamed again. Screamed and squealed so loudly that Tommo and I buried our heads in Big Bart's shoulders.

"Don't torture us, Son of God!" the demons pleaded. "Don't send us back to the dark abyss!"

"He can do that?" I whispered.

"He stopped a storm," whispered Tommo.

"What's an abyss?" whispered Bart.

"It's hell!" cried the demons. "Hell! And we don't want to go back. Send us into that herd of pigs, instead. The pigs, high up on the hill."

"Then go!" Jesus commanded. And, at once, the man relaxed and fell to the ground before him.

"Wow!" said Tommo.

"AMAZING!" I added.

"He's still naked, though," shuddered Bart. "Can we have a robe or a sheet or something over here?"

And then the squealing started again. But it wasn't coming from the man. It was coming from the top of the hill. And then it was coming down the hill, as the demon-filled pigs raced to the cliff at the hill's end and launched themselves into the air.

"Hey, Big Fella," said Tommo. "Flying pigs! Looks like you'll have to get back in that boat after all."

And then he hesitated. And then he winced. And then he said, "No. Wait. My mistake. They're not flying. They're . . . falling. And . . . landing. And . . . OOCH . . . OUCH . . . OINK . . . that's not a pretty sight."

"Well, at least the squealing's stopped," said Bart.

130

"And the shouting has just begun," I said. "Look."

A whole crowd of people were running towards us, arms waving, voices raised, and a very angry, red-faced man leading the way.

"I suspect that's the man who owns the pigs," said Jesus.

"Followed by most of his neighbours and friends," I added. "I wonder how they knew it was our fault?"

"DEMONS!" Tommo muttered. "Dirty rotten snitches!"

"Well, I think it really is time to go, now," said Jesus. "Everybody back in the boat."

Tommo looked at Big Bart. "And he does mean everybody."

132

"No argument here," said Bart.

"But what about him?" I asked, pointing to the man on the ground.

"I'd like to come with you," the man said, softly.

"I know you would," said Jesus. "But I've got something more important for you to do. Some of those people are angry. Some of them are Scared. I need someone who knows them to stay behind and tell them what happened here, so they'll be amazed, instead, and give thanks to God for what he has done for you. Is that all right?"

"It is," said the man.

"Thank you," said Jesus.

And we all climbed into the boat and waved goodbye.

"He was nice," said Bart, as we sailed away from the shore.

"Yeah," I nodded. "In a naked-chain-dangling-no-more-demons-inside sort of way."

"So what now?" asked Tommo.

"Hard to say," I shrugged. "More ups and downs I guess. Like I said, this 'Following Jesus' thing is full of surprises. We've learnt a bit about catering, a bit about being nice to Romans . . ."

"A bit about plastering," added Tommo.

"And a lot about losing your lunch," belched Bart.

"And now demons and graveyards and self-destructing pigs!" I said. "It can't get any tougher than this!"

"I don't know about that," said Jesus. "There's a lot of evil left in this world. We're going to Jerusalem, one day, and all of this will seem like a picnic compared to that."

"Jerusalem?" said Bart. "I like Jerusalem."

"Me too," said Tommo.

"Are we going soon?" I asked.

"Soon enough," said Jesus, as he settled himself down and shut his eyes. "Soon enough. But now we need some rest." And Tommo and Big Bart and I shut our eyes, too, as the ship sailed back across the lake.

Chapter 8

TAX

"When you give them your money,
they never give you anything back!"

Jesus jumped out of the boat and waded to shore. And so did we – his disciples – with Tommo, Big Bart and me bringing up the rear.

"It's good to be back," I grinned. "Back in Capernaum-by-the Sea!"

"But what a trip!" sighed Bart. "There was that big storm, for a start."

"And that crazy, naked demon guy. And that angry mob. And those suicidal pigs," added Tommo.

"Where did Jesus say we were going next?" asked Bart.

"To see the tax collector," I said.

"He didn't happen to say WHICH tax collector, did he?" asked Tommo.

"No, why?" I asked.

"No reason," Tommo shrugged. "Just curious."

"I hate tax collectors," said Bart.

"Me too," I grunted. "They're cheats, you know. They take lots more than they're supposed to, and just keep the extra for themselves."

"And they're traitors," added Tommo. "They work for the Romans."

Bart looked amazed. "I did not know any of that," he admitted.

"Then why do you hate them?" I asked.

"It's obvious, isn't it?" Bart shrugged. "When you give them your money, they never give you anything back! At every other stall in the

market-place, you give the man your money and you get a blanket or a coat or a juicy slice of goat-on-a-stick.

But when the tax collector takes your money, you get nothing. Not even a thank you."

"What's obvious, Bart," Tommo sighed, "is that you have no idea what a tax collector does or how the tax system works."

"Yeah, Big Fella," I agreed. "You don't get anything back because they use that money to build things – like roads and bridges."

"And palaces. And fortresses," Tommo added. "And armies. To enslave and oppress our people. Like I said: traitors."

Bart scratched his head. "So why don't we just stop giving them the money?"

And both Tommo and I sighed.

"Because they would kill us," Tommo explained.

"I see," Bart nodded. "That's a fair trade. We give them money and they don't kill us. Now I understand how the tax system works!"

"And look," I said, "there's the tax collector. He's talking to Jesus."

Bart waved. I sighed again. And Tommo disappeared.

"He's hiding behind me," Bart whispered to me. So I slipped quietly behind Bart,

too, and whispered, "What's the problem, Tommo? You don't, by any chance, owe that man money, do you?"

"Could do," said Tommo. "Might do. Probably do."

"Well, you could pay it to him now!" Bart whispered. And then he added, "Why are we whispering?"

"Because I do not have the money to pay him," Tommo explained. "And I do not want him to see me. Or the thugs standing behind him either."

"Because they will kill you!" Bart exclaimed. "I'm catching on, aren't I?"

"SHHHHH!" Tommo and I shushed together.

"This is **serious**!" said Tommo. "That tax collector's name is Matthew – and he is the worst! You know how people are always complaining that their taxes are costing them an arm and a leg? Well, you don't pay Matthew and he sends his goons around to **break** things. And an arm and a leg is usually where they start!"

Bart put a finger to his chin. "So they don't kill you right away," he concluded. "Just a bit at a time. That's fair."

"**IT'S NOT FAIR**!" I protested. "It's all about forcing as much money out of you as they can. That Matthew has grown rich on other people's suffering. He ought to be ashamed."

Just then, Jesus turned to face us.

"I have good news!" he announced. "I have been talking with Matthew, here, and he has decided to join us. Say hello to my newest disciple!"

"I'm shocked," I said.

"I'm puzzled," said Bart.

"I'm doomed," whimpered Tommo.

"What's more," Jesus continued, "he has invited all of us to his house tonight for a slap-up meal. He wants us to meet his friends. So get yourselves ready, and I'll see you at Matthew's place for dinner!"

The disciples wandered away in every direction, but Tommo and Bart and I wandered away the fastest! And when we were out of sight of the tax collector's booth, Tommo turned to us and said,

"I'm not going! I CAN'T GO! That's all there is to it."

"But Jesus asked us to go!" said Bart, "so we have to. We're supposed to follow him wherever he leads us."

"That's easy for you to say," Tommo groaned. "He's not leading you to a certain and painful death!"

"I think that's a little **extreme**, Tommo," I said. "I mean, if Matthew is following Jesus too – if he's one of us now – then he's hardly going to break your legs."

"But what about his friends?" Tommo argued. "I owe him money. He owes them money. So maybe they decide to collect from me. Did you see the size of the goons that were with him? What if they've been invited too?"

Bart smiled. "**Goons**. I like that word. **Goons**."

"You're not helping," I muttered.

"I beg to differ," said Bart. "I am helping. For I have already come up with a brilliant plan!"

Tommo shook his head. "**Brilliant**. **Plan**. **Bart**. Three words that do not usually go together."

But Bart would not be deterred. "That's because you have never met my Aunt Athalia. She was a master of disguise!"

"Do tell," I sighed, "because you're going to do it anyway."

"She was so good," Bart explained, "that none of us ever knew what she really looked like! A beautiful maiden, one day. A horrible hag, the next. A cow. A goose. A cactus. She could make herself look like anything!"

"And she did this because . . .?" I asked.

"Because it was her hobby!" Bart grinned. "Everyone needs a hobby. That's what her husband, Uncle Hedediah, used to say. His hobby was dirt."

"WHAT? Making things **out of** dirt?" asked Tommo. "Searching for things **in** dirt?"

"No. Just dirt," said Bart. "He had an amazing collection; kept most of it on his body."

"So if we go to your aunt Athalia," I suggested, "she'll make a disguise for Tommo."

"Not likely," said Bart. "Aunt Athalia has been gone for many years. It's a sad story. She was disguised as a baby bunny. A cute and cuddly little thing. An amazing costume. She was crossing the road, just minding her own

business, when an eagle _swooped_ down from the sky, plucked her up in its powerful talons and carried her away."

"That **is** a sad story," Tommo agreed. "So your aunt was eaten by an eagle."

"I didn't say she was **eaten!**" Bart protested. "I just said she was **gone**. She sent us a letter, many years later, explaining everything – how the eagle had carried her to its nest, and upon discovering its mistake, promptly kicked her out, from whence she stumbled unharmed into the nearest village."

"So she never came back?" I asked.

"Her husband was covered with dirt," Bart shrugged. "Would **you**?"

"So how does any of this information **help**?" cried Tommo.

"Because," Bart explained, "Aunt Athalia passed on to me, her favourite nephew, many of her costume-making secrets. You heard right, Tommo. I, Big Bart, will provide you with a disguise tonight. And not even your nearest and dearest friends will be able to recognise you."

When the sun had set and the cool evening had arrived, Jesus and the rest of us made our separate ways to Matthew's house. Tommo, Bart and I were a little late. "This is Not going to work," groaned Tommo. "I can feel it!"

"I'm sorry, kind stranger, did you say something?" asked Bart. "And why do you walk so closely to my friend and me?"

"Give it a rest Bart," I sighed. "You know perfectly well that it's Tommo!"

"It sounds like Tommo," Bart agreed. "But it looks like someone I have never seen before – so amazing is his disguise!"

"I think that's pushing it, Big Fella," I said. "All you gave him was a mudbeard."

"Ahh, but what a beautiful mudbeard it is!" Bart said, proudly. "Look at the detailed work, the fine curlicues at the end. See, you can pick out every piece of hair!"

"I think I can pick out bits of straw as well," grumbled Tommo. "Where did you say you got this mud?"

"Don't pick at it!" Bart scolded. "You'll ruin the effect!"

"But I can hardly move my mouth," Tommo complained. "And it smells kinda funny. Are you sure this is mud?"

"My dear Tommo," Bart sighed. "A true artist can fashion a masterpiece from any medium. The source of the mud. What is mixed in the mud. Where I found the mud. Who did what in the mud. All of that is irrelevant. It is only the finished product that counts!"

"Whatever you say," sighed Tommo. "Let's just get in there and hope for the best."

But before we could enter Matthew's house, we were approached by a couple of religious leaders.

"You there, $TOp!" called the first religious leader. "We want to talk to you!"

"THAT'S RIGHT, YOU THREE!" called the second. "The big one and the little one. And the one with the mudbeard."

"I'm worried," Bart whispered.

"I'm sure it will be fine," I whispered back.

"I am utterly and completely doomed," whispered Tommo.

"You are Jesus' disciples, are you not?" said the first religious leader, like he was making an accusation.

"That's right," I nodded.

"So why are you and your master eating at the house of a notorious sinner like Matthew?" asked the second.

"The question had kind of occurred to us as well," Tommo admitted.

"But we're late for dinner," added Bart.

"So we'll ask Jesus – and let you know," I offered.

And we shuffled past the religious leaders and into the house.

We were the last guests to arrive, so there were only three seats left, bunched together between two of Matthew's friends.

"I'm not sitting next to the goon," Tommo whispered, as we made our way around the table.

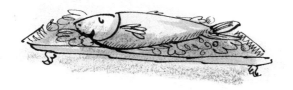

"Goon," Bart chuckled. "I do love that word."

"Then you can sit next to him," Tommo
grunted. "And Pip can sit next to you. And I will
then be as far away from him as possible!"

"Sounds good to me," I said. And we sat
ourselves down and joined in the meal.

It was an amazing spread. And Bart grinned
as he glanced around the table.

"My favourite food groups!" he exclaimed. "The cake group. The pie group. And the goat group." And he grabbed himself a handful of each and piled them on his plate. Then he turned to me and asked, "What are you having?"

"A mixture of food I can actually live on," I said. "You know, the odd vegetable. That sort of thing."

"Each to his own!" Bart smiled. But when he turned to eat what was on his plate, it was gone!

"HEY!" he shouted. "Where'd my grub go?" Then he looked at the goon who was sitting next to him. Cake crumbs covered his face, and there was the tip of a crunchy goat tail dangling from his mouth.

"PIP!" Bart whispered. "PIP! The guy sitting next to me swiped my grub!"

"So tell him to stop it," I shrugged.

"Have you seen the size of him?" Bart said. "He's three times as big as me! And I remember what Tommo said about that 'arm and leg' thing. I like my arms. And my legs."

"Then just take some more!" I said. "He can't possibly eat all your food!"

Tommo, meanwhile, was keeping his head down and chewing as little as possible, for fear that his mudbeard would crack and fall off. The attractive woman sitting next to him, however, would not leave him alone.

"You eat like a bird," she cooed. "I like that in a man. And I like a nicely trimmed beard as well!"

"Thank you," Tommo muttered. "That's . . . that's very kind."

"I've never seen a beard like that!" she continued. "So finely combed. And the smell? What sort of oils do you use?"

"It's a . . . secret mixture," he answered. "Courtesy of my friend over there. I'll ask him if you like."

But Bart had plenty more problems of his own.

"He did it AGAIN!" Bart whispered to me. "He swiped my grub!"

"Well, I don't know what you expect me to do," I grumbled. "If I say something he's likely to eat me too!"

So Bart tried to keep the goon from touching his food, while Tommo struggled to keep the pretty lady from touching his beard. And by the end of the meal, neither had succeeded.

"GOOD GRUB!" grunted the goon. And he patted Bart on the back, nearly knocking him to the floor.

"GOOD GRACIOUS!" exclaimed the pretty lady. "That beard is as hard as a rock! You

 must use some amazing gel!"

And as we left, we talked together about Matthew's dinner.

"I got really full," I said.

"I got a date!" grinned Tommo.

"I got really hungry," sighed Bart. "But then I got a new friend. Seems that his arms were really sore. Apparently, that 'breaking legs' thing

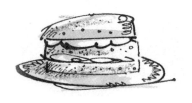

takes a lot out of you. He thought I was simply getting his food for him, so he wouldn't have to reach so far. He was very grateful. So if WE ever need anybody's legs breaking . . ."

"I don't think that's likely," I said. "But I'm glad it all worked out for you."

"And I'm glad that the three of you got on so well with the guests around you," said Jesus, who had walked up behind us.

"That reminds me,
Jesus," I said. "We met

a couple of religious leaders as we were coming
in. They had a question."

"Yeah," Bart nodded. "They wanted to know
why you ate with sinners."

Jesus smiled. "They would, wouldn't they?
How would you answer them?"

"Well, if by sinners," Bart answered, "you
mean Gordon—"

"Gordon?" I asked.

"Yeah. Gordon the Goon," Bart shrugged.

"The goon?" asked Jesus.

"That's what he said his name was. Gordon
the Goon. Who was I to argue? Anyway, if by
sinners you mean Gordon, then I would say

165

that if I had not talked to him, then I would not have discovered what a nice fellow he was."

"But he ate ALL your cakes!" I reminded him.

"True," Bart nodded. "But I would probably have done the same thing if I had been in his enormous shoes."

"That's good, Bart," Jesus grinned. "I think I would also have said that you send a doctor to somebody who needs to be healed, not to someone who is already well. So if somebody needs a bad habit fixing—"

"Like swiping every cake in sight," Bart suggested.

"Like thievery or gluttony," Jesus agreed, "then that's who I am going to spend my time with.

Nice mudbeard, by the way, Tommo," Jesus
added.

"Thank you, Jesus," Tommo sighed.

"Which brings me to Matthew. And his
former job. And your former debt."

"Former?" asked Tommo hopefully.

"**That's right**," Jesus smiled. "You see, what needed fixing in Matthew was his greed, his dishonesty, and his tendency to resort to leg-breaking if he didn't get his way – all of which he has promised to leave behind, now that he is following me."

"So I'm off the HOOK?" asked Tommo.

"You're off the hook," Jesus grinned.

"**Which means** . . .?" asked Tommo.

"Which means you can wash off that beard," Jesus answered. Then he wrinkled his nose. "And are you **sure** it's made of mud?"

Chapter 9

SLEEP

"Need pillow. Need bed.
Need one massive long nap!"

Bart yawned. Bart yawned again. Bart yawned a third time.

"We keeping you up, Big Man?" Tommo grunted.

"No-aaaaah," Bart yawned a fourth time. "I was out with Matthew and some of his mates last night. We got in really late."

Then he yawned a fifth time and stretched his Big Bart arms. "I just want to go to sleep."

"There's no time for that," said Tommo. "Jesus says we have a really busy day ahead of us. Just keep walking."

"**Can't**," Bart yawned again. "Need pillow. Need bed. Need one massive long nap!" And he stretched and he yawned one more time, just to make the point. I reached up and tapped him on the shoulder.

"I think you're gonna have to put that nap on hold, Big Fella. L∞k."

Sure enough, a huge crowd was making its way toward Jesus and the rest of us. And at the front of the crowd was a very official-looking man.

"Hey, I know him!" I said. "His name is Jairus. He runs the local synagogue."

"I could use a synagogue about now," Bart yawned. "A little praying. A little preaching. Puts me right to sleep."

"No, No, he's very good," I objected. "And he's a friend of my cousin Sam. Used to have us over for dinner all the time. He has a really nice family.

"**Very interesting**," Bart yawned again. "So interesting that I might just fall asleep where I'm standing."

As soon as he reached Jesus, Jairus fell to his knees.

"**Please** help my daughter," he begged. "She's only twelve. She's all I have. And she's dying."

"OMIGOSH!" I said. "Did you hear that? Jesus has got to do something!"

And so Jesus did.

"C'mon, lads," he called to all of us – and we set off right away, pushing back through the crowd.

"Don't worry!" said Tommo. "Jesus will sort it."

"I certainly hope so," I said.

"And then we can have that nap!" added Bart, rubbing his eyes.

But almost as soon as he'd started, Jesus stopped. And he looked around. And he asked a question.

"Who touched me?"

Bart looked at Tommo. Tommo looked at me.

I looked at Bart. We all looked puzzled as we were all thinking **exactly** the same thing.

Who touched you? A gazillion people – that's who!

But it was Peter who actually said something.

"Teacher," he said, "look at the crowd. There are people all around you!"

Jesus nodded. "I know. But this was different. It wasn't a bump or a nudge or any kind of casual contact. Somebody touched me because they needed my help. And I felt the healing power of God flow out of me."

"**WOW**!" wowed Tommo. "That's **amazing!**"

"Yeah," I added. "But what about Jairus's daughter?"

"WHaaaat?" yawned Bart. He could hardly keep awake.

"Stay with us, Big Fella!" I said.

"Jesus is doing his miracle thing again. But he'd better hurry."

"I knooooow," Bart yawned once more. "I'm sooo sleepy. And we still have to go to that synagogue guy's house. I'll never get my nap."

Just then, a woman fell trembling at Jesus' feet.

"It was me," she admitted. "I'm the one who touched you. I've had a problem with bleeding for twelve years. I've spent all my money on doctors. But no one has been able to heal me.

Well, not until now. Because when I touched you, the bleeding stopped!"

The crowd cheered. Jesus smiled. Then he took her hand, lifted her to her feet, and said,

"It's your faith – the trust you put in me and in God's power – that has healed you. Go in peace."

Everyone was happy. Jesus. The woman. The crowd. Everyone but Jairus, who was looking more worried than ever. And me.

"C'MON! C'MON!" I whispered. "We've got to get going!" And then I saw someone pushing through the crowd – pushing right towards us.

"Hey!" I said. "That's my cousin! That's Sam!"

And I jumped up and down and shouted and waved.

But Sam paid me no attention. No attention at all. He was looking straight at Jairus. And his look was not a happy one.

"Jairus," said Sam, **huffing** and **puffing** to catch his breath and trying his best to hold back his tears.

"Your daughter . . ." Sam continued, and he couldn't even bring himself to say her name. "Your daughter is dead. There's no need for Jesus to come."

The whole crowd went quiet. Bart stopped his yawning. And I rubbed the corner of one eye.

"You got something stuck in there?" said Bart.

"Can't you see he's upset?" whispered Tommo.

"Shut up. Both of you," I sniffled. And then I sighed and added, "Jesus heals other people.

Stupid, naked demon guys. People we don't even know. How come he doesn't heal our friends?"

Jesus looked at Jairus. He was very serious.

"**Don't be afraid**," he said. "Trust me – like that woman did – and your daughter will be healed too."

"SEE?" said Tommo, his hand on my shoulder. "Jesus is going to heal her."

"But she's already dead!" I sighed. "That's what Sam said."

Bart scratched his head, remembering.

"But so was that boy. The one from Nain. He was already in his coffin, and Jesus brought him back from the dead."

"So maybe he can do the same with the girl!"
said Tommo. "**C'mon**, let's go." Tommo and
Bart and I followed the crowd to Jairus's house.
But when we arrived, all we could hear was
weeping and wailing.

Bart shook his head sadly. "Professional mourners. You don't hire them unless you're sure. Looks like Sam was right, Pip. The girl really is dead."

But Jesus had a different opinion.

"Why all the fuss?" he said to the crowd. "The girl isn't dead. She's only sleeping."

And at once the weeping turned into mocking laughter.

"YEAH, RIGHT!"

"That's what you say."

"Pull the other one, Jesus."

"Uh-oh," whispered Tommo. "That didn't go down well."

"They're upset!" I said. "What do you expect?"

"Sleep," yawned Bart. "At least someone gets to sleep."

And then he scRatcHed his head again.

"So is she really asleep? Or is she dead? Or is she just dead tired? Or is she sleeping the sleep of the dead? Or is Jesus just saying she's asleep, because she's really dead and . . . and . . ."

"And he means to wake her up!" grinned Tommo. "Like he did with the boy from Nain."

"That's what I'm hoping," I said, softly. "But it's a lot to hope for."

"Then let's go and see!" said Bart.

But before we could step into the house, Jesus pointed at Peter, James, and John.

"You three," he said. "Come with me. The rest of you – stay out here." And along with Jairus and his wife, Jesus and Peter and James and John went into the house.

"Flippin' fishermen!" grumbled Tommo. "They always get the best jobs."

"Peter, James and John. Teacher's pets," moaned Bart.

"SAM!" I shouted. "OVER HERE!" And my cousin saw me and came running and gave me a big hug.

"That's amazing!" said Tommo. "He's little, like you are, Pip. You could be twins, in fact, except that Sam is—"

"Even hairier," observed Bart. "You look a lot like Pip, except you're a whole lot hairier."

"It's from our grandmother's side,"
chuckled Sam, his voice much like mine too.
"Hairy heads. Hairy beards. Hairy arms. And
look, we've even got hair on our toes!"

"Impressive," grunted Tommo, but he didn't sound impressed at all. "Oh, and sorry about your friend."

"**Mary**?" Sam sighed. "Yeah. I certainly hope Jesus can do something. But, to be honest, I think it's too late." And then he started rubbing the corner of his eye, much like I had done earlier.

"We were inseparable when we were kids. Pip'll tell you. Mary was younger, yeah, but she followed us wherever we went."

And I just nodded and sighed, "Sam, Mary and Pip. What adventures we had!"

"I wish we could go in there and see what's happening," said Bart.

"Jesus told us not to," Tommo reminded him.

"But he didn't tell me," grinned Sam. "There's a window round the back. It's kind of high off the ground, but if someone could give me a leg up . . ." And he looked at Bart and winked.

"Yeah, that would be handy . . ." Bart mused. And then the denarius dropped. "Oh, you mean me? Yeah. Of course."

"We can all help!" I offered. "If you promise to tell us what you see in there."

So, forming a sort of human set of steps, Bart knelt down on all fours in front of the window, Tommo knelt behind him, I knelt behind Tommo, and Sam bounded up on our backs, one-two-three, and stuck his hairy head above the windowsill.

"They're all in the room," he whispered. "Jesus' back is to me. He's leaning over the bed. I'm looking straight at Mary and she's just lying there.

She doesn't look good. Now Jesus is taking her hand. And he's saying something. Sounds like . . . sounds like . . . 'Little girl, get up!' And she

is! I mean, she's up! She's awake! She's not
dead!"

And I jumped up for joy. And so did Tommo.
And so did Big Bart! And Sam went shooting up
into the air and past the window! He said he
caught Mary's eye on the way down and she

laughed at the sight of him flying by, but no one else inside was any the wiser because they were all looking at her and were so happy that she was alive!

A great big dinner followed. Rumour had it that it was Jesus' idea, on Mary's behalf, the theory being that being dead, or being asleep, or whatever, works up quite an appetite.

But when we gathered round the table, someone was missing.

"Where's Bart?" asked Jesus. "Can't imagine **him** missing a meal." And then we heard something. Something out the back. Something that sounded like **snoring**.

And when Tommo and Sam and I looked out of the window, there was Bart, his back propped up against the house, his head lolling to one side, and his mouth wide open.

"Looks like he's asleep," I said.

"Looks like he's dead," grunted Tommo.

"Dead? Asleep?" grinned Sam. "When Jesus is around, it doesn't seem to **matter**!"

Chapter 10

FOOD

"There is always more
than enough to go around."

"What was that?" Tommo grunted.

"What?" asked Bart.

"That noise?"

Bart shrugged. "I didn't hear anything."

"Well, I did," I said. "It sounded like a wolf. A wolf devouring a sheep."

"Or maybe strangling it," noted Tommo. "Yeah. Definitely. Strangling. A ravenous wolf and a strangled sheep."

"And a duck," I added. "I think I heard a duck as well. A deranged duck, with one mad eye, as it smacks into a tree."

"Hmm," Bart nodded. "A ravenous wolf. A strangled sheep. A deranged duck. That would be my stomach. I'm **famished**!"

"Me, too," I sighed.

"Well, we've been here all day!" said Tommo. "Jesus has taught some good stuff. And he's healed people. It takes time. What do you expect?"

"A LUNCH BREAK!" said Bart. "But then, I didn't actually bring any lunch."

"I don't think anybody did," I said. "Listen, there are plenty more deranged ducks and strangled sheep out there in the crowd. We aren't the only ones who are hungry."

"Makes you think about food, though, doesn't it?" said Tommo, dreamily. "Like a big pot of lamb stew."

"Stop it!" cried Bart, shoving his fingers into his ears.

"Makes you even hungrier, doesn't it, Big Fella?" I said.

"No, it makes me ILL!" Big Bart choked. "The lumpy lamby bits get stuck in your throat and make you gag! It's horrible!"

"So I guess it's chicken stew for you, then," I suggested.

Bart turned green. "**Chicken Stew!**" he cringed. "That's even worse! When she was expecting me, my mum was frightened by a rabid rooster. I get hives if I even smell a chicken."

"**WOW!**" I said. "I did not know that. I have obviously not been paying attention to your diet. So you're a vegetarian, then?"

And Bart just howled. "Veggies? *Noooo!* I can't stand veggies. And there's a broccoli-shaped rash on my bum to prove it!"

"So what can you eat, Big Fella?" Tommo asked.

"Cakes, mostly," Bart smiled. "And pies. And sweets. And goat-on-a-stick."

"Well, that explains the belly, doesn't it?" Tommo sighed.

"Hey! I'm big-boned," Bart protested.

"And big-bottomed," I chuckled. "Sorry."

Just then, Jesus walked by.

"The crowd's getting hungry, lads," he said. "You can almost hear their stomachs grumbling."

"Ravenous wolves," muttered Tommo.

"Strangled sheep," I added.

"Something about one-eyed ducks," Bart concluded.

"If you say so," answered Jesus, puzzled. "But the question is, where are we going to buy food for all of them?"

"Buy food?" I laughed. "For all these people? It's just a guess, but I reckon it would cost something like eight months' wages!"

"And that's on good pay," added Tommo, "with overtime."

"And even then," Bart concluded, "no one would get more than an itsy-bitsy, teeny-weeny, bite-sized little bit. There's no way we can feed all these people. It's a joke, right?"

198

But Jesus wasn't laughing.

"Just thought it would be helpful for us to understand the scale of the problem," he grinned.

"And . . .?" I asked.

"And here's Andrew!" Jesus announced, "with the beginning of a solution!"

Andrew had a boy with him. The boy had a basket. And in the basket were five small loaves of barley bread and two little fish."

"It's not much of a beginning," shrugged Tommo.

"No," Jesus smiled. "But then neither was the water in those jars before I turned it into wine."

"**Point taken**," said Tommo. "So you're going to turn the fish and bread into . . .**wine?**"

"No. Just more fish and bread, I think," said Jesus. And he bowed his head and said, "Thank you for this food, Father. Make it enough to feed this crowd. Teach us to share and help us to see

that, with your help, there is always more than enough to go around."

Then he opened his eyes and started breaking off chunks of fish and bread. And the more he broke off, the more there was!

"That's aMaZ_iNg!" cried Tommo.

"Another miracle!" I shouted.

But Bart just sat there, shaking and shivering . . . and scratching.

"Fish-itch. Fish-itch. Fish-itch," he repeated, over and over again.

"Sorry, Jesus," I apologised. "Bart has a whole mess of dietary issues. And it looks like he's allergic to fish as well."

"No problem," said Jesus. "You two help the others pass out the food, and I'll find something else for Bart to do."

So Tommo and I grabbed as much fish and bread as we could carry and started passing it round. Up and down and back and forth across the hillside we went. And the crowd was **thrilled**!

Bart, meanwhile, was sent to talk to one of Jesus' other disciples, Matthew, who gave him a fish-free assignment. And that's what he was doing, when Tommo and I came back for another load of food.

"**So** what are you up to, Big Fella?" I asked.

"A completely impossible job," Bart sighed, "that's what."

"Well, at least you're not itching," said Tommo.

"No, but my head hurts," Bart moaned. "You know how Matthew is always writing stuff down, what we do and what Jesus says – a bit

like you and your diary, Pip. Well, he thinks it would be helpful if we knew how many people were being fed today."

"There's **gazillions!**" I said.

"That's what I told him," Bart explained. "But he said 'gazillions' wasn't a real number. He wanted me to make a REAL count, with PROPER numbers – so he'd know how many there were."

"That's rough," Tommo grunted.

"You're telling me," Bart sighed again. "I started with the kids. But they take a bite and then they run around. So they're here, they're there. You don't know if you've counted the same kid once or twice or **six** times! And their mums are no better. They keep running after them, shouting at them to finish their lunch."

"So just count the men," I suggested. "They're all sitting down, nice and still, stuffing their faces. That'll be eaSy. And then just say there were some women and children too."

A huge smile broke out across Bart's face.

"Pip, you are a GENIUS! I would give you a big hug, except that you smell like fish and even from here you are starting to make me retch."

"Fair enough, Big Fella," I grinned. "Looks like there's another load of grub to pass round anyway. Jesus just keeps breaking off more. His fingers must be getting really tired! We'll see you when it's all over."

So we all went back to work, and when everyone had been fed, and twelve whole baskets full of leftovers had been collected, Tommo and Big Bart and I collapsed on the hillside.

"I'm shattered," I said.

"Totally and completely **exhausted**," Tommo agreed.

"My brain hurts," added Bart. "And my fingers and my toes. I never knew counting could be so hard."

"So what's the final number?" I asked.

"Four thousand, nine hundred and eighty-seven," sighed Bart. "Best as I can figure."

"Well, at least Matthew will be pleased," Tommo grunted.

"Don't think so," said Bart. "I mean he's writing this stuff down, so I guess he wants to make it into a book someday. But it just doesn't SOUND good, does it – The Feeding of the 4,987?"

"So round it up," I suggested. "Who will know?"

"Another **genius** idea!" Bart beamed. "The Feeding of the 4,990. It has a ring to it!"

And then he hopped to his Big Bart feet.

"Where are you going?" asked Tommo.

"To tell Matthew," said Bart. And he trundled up over the crest of the hill. But no sooner had he gone than he was back again, with a boy in tow.

"Look what I **found**!" he shouted.

"Another boy?" asked Tommo.

"With another basket?" I added.

"**Exactly**!" grinned Bart. "But he doesn't have fish and bread in his basket. **Look**!" And he flung it open. "**CAKES**!"

"So you're off to see Jesus, aren't you?" sighed Tommo.

"YOU BETCHA!" Bart grinned. "This miracle isn't over. Not by a long shot. There are 4,990 people out there who need dessert!"

Chapter 11

WATER

"Hold on, everybody . . .
It's going to get bumpy!"

Big Bart crossed his arms and stood stock-still, like an enormous statue.

"I'm not going," he grunted. "Don't ask me again."

"But the boat is ready to go!" I sighed. "Everyone's waiting."

"Don't care," muttered Bart. "Not going."

"Chicken," clucked Tommo.

"Not going."

"Cluck-cluck-cluck!" I added.

"Sticks and stones," said Bart. "Not going. NOT going. NOT GOING!"

"Stop it!" I shouted. "Stop it right now! Are we going to have this exact same conversation every time we have to get into a boat?"

"Umm . . . maybe," Bart muttered.

"But it went fine the last time," argued Tommo.

"Apart from the fact that I puked up both my breakfast and my lunch, sure," Bart reminded him. "Oh, and there was the little matter of that storm. The one that almost **killed** us."

"But Jesus made the storm go away," I countered.

"And Jesus won't be going with us this time, will he?" Bart protested. "He told us to get in the boat and cross the lake, and that he was going up the mountainside to pray. Which means that if there is another storm, we will all be **doomed**! And besides," he added, "I'm hungry."

"And whose fault is that?" moaned Tommo. "Jesus just fed 5,000 people!"

"4,987 to be precise," said Bart.

"The point is that there was plenty of food to go around," I argued. "Fish and bread for everyone!"

"As I have explained," Bart explained, "I am allergic to fish. And I don't like the little crunchy bits in that kind of bread. Now, if it had been a different kind of bread . . ."

"If it had been a different kind of bread," Tommo sighed, "you would have found something wrong with that as well! If you weren't so flippin' finicky, you'd be full like the rest of us!"

"THAT'S NOT FAIR," Bart reprimanded him. "There were those cakes that belonged to that other little boy, which I would have gladly eaten.

But when I asked Jesus to break them up and pass them round, too, he just laughed. I think he thought I was joking. But I wasn't."

"Because you wanted those cakes, didn't you, Big Fella?" I grinned.

"I did," sighed Bart. "I really did."

"Well, it just so happens," I continued, "that I was looking out for you. I had a word with that boy. He gave me a couple of those cakes. And they are sitting in my bag, at this very moment!"

"That was very thoughtful," Bart grinned back. "May I have them, please?"

"Of course," I said. And I tossed the bag in Bart's direction. Or, more precisely, I threw the bag high over Bart's head, and past his grasping hands. It sailed through the air and landed in the back of the boat. And like a puppy in pursuit of a bone, Bart followed the bag, heedless of his surroundings, and finished up in the boat too!

Tommo and I hopped aboard and shouted "Shove off!" And with Bart's head buried in the bag, we set sail across the lake.

It was only when he came up for air, mouth full and face covered with crumbs, that Bart realised what had happened.

"NOT FAIR!" he sputtered, bits of cake spewing out in every direction. "You tricked me!"

"Yes," I admitted. "But at least you got your cakes."

"I'll say," grunted Tommo. "I've never seen food go down so fast."

And then the boat hit a bumpy wave. And then another and then a third. And Bart turned green.

"I think it might be coming back even faster," he gulped. And with a "Hwork!" he deposited what no longer looked much like cakes back in the bottom of my bag!

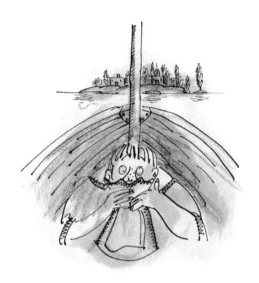

"That's my bag!" I cried.

"That's disgusting!" Tommo grunted.

"That's hilarious!" Peter howled. "He's lost his lunch again!" And Andrew and James and John laughed along with him.

"Shut up!" I shouted. "He isn't like you guys. He hasn't spent his whole life on a boat!"

And Tommo just shook his head and muttered, "Flippin' fishermen!"

"**Sorry**," Peter chuckled. "We'll try to be more understanding. It's just that he has no idea how bad it can really get out here."

"I'll say," added Andrew. "Do you remember that wave a few years back? The one that looked like a tunnel? We got through it just before it **collapsed**!"

"Or the night the mast split right in half!" said John.

"Or the time old Ebenezer got knocked off the back of the boat," James went on. "He was coughing up crayfish for a month!"

And then they all laughed out loud again.

"**THAT'S ENOUGH!**" I shouted.

"Can't you see you're making things worse?" grumbled Tommo. "Why don't you just leave us alone and go back to your . . . your . . . flippin' fisherman stuff?"

And Bart just sat there whimpering, fingers jammed in his ears, repeating over and over again, "Happy thoughts. Happy thoughts. Cakes. Happy thoughts."

I patted him on the head. Hang in there, Big Fella."

And Tommo put a hand on his shoulder.

"It'll be all right, mate."

But it wasn't. Not by a long shot.

The sun set. The moon rose. And then the clouds rolled in.

The further we sailed, the harder the wind blew. And the more difficult it got to make any progress at all.

"Looks like we're in for a rough night!" called Peter.

"Hold on, everybody!" added Andrew. "It's going to get bumpy!"

"And that means you, Landlubber Bart!" shouted John.

"You mean land-blubberer!" sniggered his brother James.

I staggered to my feet, ready to shout right back, desperate to shut them up. But there was no need. The fishermen had already fallen silent. They were looking past me, across the water. They were pointing. And they were trembling.

"What is it?" croaked Peter.

"Too small for a boat," Andrew shivered.

"Too big for a fish," quivered John.

"That's 'cos it's a person," squeaked James, as the clouds parted and the moonlight shone on the mysterious figure. "It's not a 'something' out there. It's a 'somebody'. IT'S A GHOST!"

So frightened were the fishermen, that I started to tremble too. But I had to have a look. I just had to. **Slowly** I turned round, my fingers like a fence in front of my face, one eye shut and the other peeping through the tiniest finger-fence gap.

I looked. I saw. I screamed. And then I jumped back down to where I'd been sitting and burrowed as best I could behind Bart.

"It's true!" I trembled. "It's out there, on the water. And it's coming straight for us. A ghost!"

"A ghost!" said Bart. And he opened his eyes and sat up straight, as a Big Bart smile crossed his no-longer-frightened face. "I love ghosts!"

"You mean, you've seen one?" stammered Tommo. "You've seen a ghost?"

"Well, not exactly. But my uncle Jeroboam did, and I have been dying to see one, myself, ever since. You see, he came home from a wedding party, once – a little worse for wear, if you know what I mean – and he tried to milk the donkey. The donkey was not impressed and kicked Uncle Jeroboam across the yard. He

was unconscious for a while, but when he woke up, there was the ghost!

"'JEROBOAM!' the ghost called in what my uncle says was a terrifying, high, shrieking voice. 'Forsake your wicked ways. Do not indulge in much wine!' And then he passed out again.

"It's all very spooky, and what makes things even more strange is that he says the ghost looked exactly like my Aunt Agatha. Who died. Two years later."

"Not to be **Sceptical**," Tommo said, unwilling to let even mortal dread keep him from puncturing Bart's tale. "But seeing as your aunt died two years later, is it not possible that the ghost was actually—"

"Look!" cried Bart, leaping to his feet. "I see it! I see it. There it is!"

And then he waved. "Hello, Ghosty! Nice to meet you! Why don't you come and join us?"

And, as one, the rest of us cried, "No!!!"

But the ghost did exactly what Bart asked and moved step by watery step towards the bouncing boat.

"Get us out of here!" shouted Andrew.

"It's no use!" Peter shouted back. "Can't make any headway. The wind's too strong. We're stuck!"

Head buried in hands, John cried out as well, "If only Jesus were here, he'd know what to do!"

"As it happens," said Bart, holding a finger in the air. "I think he is. That ghost doesn't look like my aunt Agatha at all. It looks like Jesus!"

And with that, a familiar and friendly voice called out across the waves.

"Have courage, lads! Don't be afraid. It's only me."

Slowly, each of us lifted up our heads and looked.

"I think Bart's right," said Andrew.

"I think it's really him!" said John.

"I think I wet myself," sighed James.

"I think I'm going to join him!" announced Peter. And he leapt right into a passing wave.

"NO!!!" we all cried again.

The wave washed by Peter and, when it had, amazingly, miraculously, he was standing on the water, just like Jesus! Slowly they moved towards each other, as though they were walking on solid ground. But then the wind began to blow again, and Peter lost his nerve and began to sink.

"Help me, Jesus!" he cried. "Save me!"

"Who's the blubberer, now?" muttered Tommo. "Flippin' Peter, that's who."

But all Jesus said was, "Why did you stop trusting me? With a little more faith, you could have done it!"

Then he held out his hand and helped Peter back into the boat. Jesus stepped on board too. And as soon as he did, the wind stopped its blowing and the waves their bouncing up and down.

Everyone cheered. Everyone but Tommo who was still moaning about 'fishermen', and Bart who looked just a little disappointed.

"What's the matter, Big Fella?" I asked.

"Aww, it's just that I was really looking forward to seeing a ghost, that's all," Bart sighed.

"But, Bart!" I cried. "You saw Jesus WALKING ON THE WATER! I'd say that's pretty impressive too."

"S'pose so," Bart admitted.

"It's more than that. It's amazing!" I said. "To think that our teacher, our friend, can do stuff like that!"

"Yeah," Tommo agreed. "In the last couple of days, he's healed a woman, raised a dead girl and turned a few chunks of fish and bread into a feast. And now this! I'd say that's more than any ordinary teacher could do."

"I'd say that's the kind of thing you'd only expect God to do!" I nodded.

"Or somebody a lot like him," said Tommo. "Like his son."

"Or . . . or . . . his nephew!" added Bart. "Like if I had seen a ghost – then I would be just the same as my uncle Jeroboam!"

"Once again," Tommo interrupted, "could I point out that your uncle didn't actually—"

But before he could finish, Peter shouted "SHOVE OFF!" And the sails filled up and the boat took off and the sudden jolt knocked the three of us back onto the floor. And, when he'd finished rubbing his head, all Tommo had left to say was, "Flippin' fishermen!"

Chapter 12

GOAT

"Not one, not two, but
three supersize portions."

"*I*'m exhausted!" Bart sighed.

"That's what you keep telling us," grunted Tommo.

"My feet hurt!" Bart moaned.

"Heard that too," I muttered.

"When are we going to—"

"ENOUGH!" Tommo and I shouted, as one.

"We told you to stop asking," said Tommo.

"We told you the last time you brought it up," I added.

"WE DO NOT KNOW WHEN WE ARE GOING TO GET THERE!" we shouted together again.

"Ha!" Bart laughed. And then he laughed a second time. "Ha! That's not what I was going to ask. So there!"

"Then what were you going to ask?" Tommo sneered.

"Ummm . . . When are . . . When are we . . . When are we . . .?" Bart tried his best to come up with a different question. He tried until his brain hurt as much as his big flat feet.

"I've got it! When are we going to know where we are going . . . to?"

"We already know!" Tommo sighed. "Jesus told us before we left. We're going to Caesarea Philippi!"

"See, that's my problem," said Bart. "I can't get my head around that name! It's too big. Too complicated."

"Then break it down," I suggested. "It starts with Caesar – like the guy who runs the Roman Empire."

"Caesar," Bart nodded. "Got it."

"And then there's a little ending – ea" I explained. "Like . . . like . . ."

"DIARRHOEA!" Bart suggested.

"All right," I sighed. "Diarrhoea."

"So it's Caesar-ea," said Bart. "And then . . .?"

"Philip," I said. "Like my real name."

"Your real name is Philip?" said Bart, amazed. "I did not know that! I always thought that Pip was short for Pippin. Or Pippi. Or Pippopotamus."

And then he put one finger to his chin, considering the situation. "Philip? Hᴍᴍ."

"And then just add 'pie'," I said. "Like I was in a pie. Like a Philip-pie. Philippi!"

Bart smiled. "I like pie. But I like meat in my pie. Or fruit. Or goat. I think that if I ate a Philip Pie it would make me ill. I'd probably end up with a horrible disease – like **Caesar-ea**."

"So have you got it?" asked Tommo.

"I think so," Bart answered. "We are going to Caesarea Philippi!" And then he added, "So when are we going to get there?"

But before we could tell him to 'stop asking' yet again, Jesus held up his hand and said,

"I've got a question! Something for you to think about while we walk."

"Excellent!" Bart whispered. "A quiz! That'll pass the time. **I spy with my little eye**, something that begins wiiiiith . . . F!"

Tommo whispered back. "I don't think that's what Jesus has in mind."

"But it's a good question," answered Bart. "Go on, see if you can figure it out."

"I don't know," sighed Tommo, looking around. "Fig tree? Fountain? Fork in the road?"

Bart giggled and pointed at me. "No, it's him! PHILIP!"

"But Philip doesn't begin with . . . oh, never mind," I groaned.

"I said, I have a question," Jesus repeated. "Assuming everyone is listening . . ."

And Bart turned to me and went "SHH!"

"We've been travelling round together for a while, now," Jesus continued. "You've listened to me teach. You've seen the miracles. And you've talked with the people in the places we've visited. So what do they think we're up to? Who do they think I am?"

There was a long pause. And a lot of humming and hawing and head-scratching. And then we walked past a street vendor. "Oooh, look!" Bart whispered. "He's selling food. He's got goat-on-a-stick! That's my favourite."

"But we're supposed to be thinking about the question," I protested.

"I don't know the answer," Bart shrugged. "And I don't talk to anybody but you two. Well, and myself, occasionally. So I'm not likely to be of any help.

"But what I do know is that I'm hungry, and I'm tired. So I'll just stay behind and have a little goaty treat. Then catch up with you in a bit. Okay?"

And before we could say "No!" or "Don't!" or "Hang on a Minute!" Bart had slipped away.

"Got to admit," admitted Tommo, "I don't know the answer, either."

But James did. He put up his hand and he spoke.

"Some people think you're John the Baptist."

"That's a bit of a stretch," Tommo whispered to me. "John the Baptist is dead."

But Jesus had very good hearing.

"You're right, Tommo," he nodded. "John is dead. Executed by King Herod because he dared to criticise the king's behaviour. You can get into trouble when you stand up against what's wrong."

Jesus looked very sad.

"He was my cousin, you know – on my mum's side. Just six months older than me.

Sent by God to tell the world that I was coming. I miss him."

Everything went quiet for a bit, and then someone else put his hand up. It was Thaddeus.

"Some people say you're a prophet, Jesus. Elijah, maybe."

Jesus smiled. "A prophet. God's messenger. And Elijah was a good one. A bit like John, in a way – standing up for what was right against another evil and corrupt king – a long, LONG time ago."

"He went to heaven in a fiery chariot, didn't he?" I said.

"So he did," Jesus grinned. "And I suppose that's why people think I might be him. Elijah come back again! It's a better guess, but hey, if I had a chariot of fire, we wouldn't have to do all this walking! So I think it will have to be 'no' to that one as well."

Everybody chuckled, and then there were more suggestions – Jeremiah, or one of the other prophets.

"Look," Jesus said at last. "It's interesting to hear what other people have to say, but I suppose the more important question is this: who do YOU think that I am?"

246

Things went quiet again. And that was followed by a lot more whispering.

"Not sure what to say," I whispered.

"Well, you know what I think," Tommo whispered back.

"You said if from the start," I answered. "You think he's the Messiah, right?"

Tommo nodded, "The Special One. The Chosen One. Sent by God to defeat our enemies, the Romans, and give us back our land again. That's what I'm hoping for, anyway."

I scratched my head. "But there's more to him than that," I said. "He does things we never heard that the Messiah would do. He feeds thousands of people with a boy's lunch. He stills storms. He walks on water! That's more

247

than Messiah stuff. That's . . . that's God stuff! But surely, he can't possibly be . . ."

And that's when Bart returned.

"GREETINGS LADS!" he said. "And look at what I've got. Not one, not two, but three supersize portions of goat-on-a-stick. And an extra-large bottle of goat juice, to boot! Never say that your buddy Bart doesn't know how to take care of his friends."

And then he passed them round. "One for Tommo. One for . . . PHILIP."

"That's nice, Bart. Thanks," I said. "But we're kind of busy, right now. Jesus just changed the question."

"Yeah," Tommo added. "He wants to know who WE think he is."

"Well, why didn't he ask that in the first place?" Bart shrugged. "It's obvious, isn't it? He's the Messiah. The Son of God."

"Well, say something, then!" I spluttered.

"Put you hand up," said Tommo, grabbing Bart's arm and hoisting it in the air."

"Careful," said Bart. "You'll spill the goat juice!"

And that's when Peter spoke.

"You are the MESSIAH," he announced. "The Son of the living God."

"Hey, that's what I said," Bart whispered.

"I know, I know," I nodded.

"Flippin' fishermen," grumbled Tommo.

But Jesus was really pleased. He told Peter that he was right. That he knew who Jesus was because he'd heard it from God. And that Peter was going to have a very important job to do.

"Listen to **that**!" Tommo groaned. "It sounds like he's putting him in charge of the rest of us."

"Yeah, that could have been you, Big Fella," I sighed.

"Doesn't bother me," Bart shrugged. "I don't think I'm cut out for that sort of thing. At least I know I had the right answer."

"And we know that Jesus is the Messiah!" Tommo grinned. "And that means goodbye to

the Romans, because OUR teacher and OUR friend – the one who stilled a storm and walked on water – is going to use his power to kick them out forever!"

"There's just one more thing," said Jesus, turning to speak to us all again. "Remember what I told you about John and Elijah? When you stand up for what's right and stand against what is evil, there's usually a price to pay.

"King Ahab tried to kill Elijah. King Herod had John put to death. I want you to know that when our time together is over, when I have taught you all I can, that my enemies will try to kill me too. And they will succeed."

"What did he say?" I asked.

"I think he said that his enemies are going to kill him," said Bart.

Tommo shook his head. "No! No! No! That's not how it's supposed to work. The Messiah is supposed to defeat his enemies. He's supposed to KILL them!"

Bart stuck a finger in his ear and wiggled it about. "Well that's what I heard," he shrugged.

"Then somebody had better talk to him!" said Tommo. "This is all wrong!"

I pointed. "Look! Peter's getting up. He's walking over to Jesus. Maybe he'll talk to him."

And then Bart stood up too.

"I know you got the answer right, Big Fella," Tommo nodded. "But I don't think you're the one to do this job."

"Me neither," Bart answered. "I just thought they might be hungry – that they'd like a bit of goat . . ."

"Don't think so, Bart," I said.

But the big man was already gone. He walked over to Peter and Jesus. He held out his stick. And just as quickly walked back again.

"Not hungry?" I asked.

"Not happy," said Bart, shaking his head. "You were right about that. Peter told Jesus just what you said, Tommo. And Jesus got really mad. He said that Peter had been listening to the **devil**, and that he wasn't being very helpful. That Jesus had to do what God wanted him to – no matter how hard it was."

Tommo shook his head too. "Good thing I didn't go over there."

"Yeah," I said. "It seems that Peter listened to God and the devil, both in one day."

"Hey, it happens," Tommo said.

"Not to me," Bart grinned. "I mostly listen to my stomach. And that's another reason I'm glad I'm not Peter."

"**WHY?**" asked Tommo.

"Because I've got something he hasn't got," Bart answered.

"What's that, Big Fella?" I asked.

And Bart grinned and held his lunch high.

"**Goat-on-a-stick!**"

Chapter 13

BUTTERFLY

"There's a first
time for everything."

*T*ommo, Big Bart and I were lying on the mountainside, hands behind our heads, staring up into the sky.

"A⊦⊦⊦⊦!" Bart sighed happily. Rest, at last."

"Couldn't agree with you more, Big Fella," said Tommo.

"A well-deserved break, if there ever was one," I agreed.

And then I started to wiggle and wriggle and yelp. And finally I jumped to my feet and started scratching.

"There's something biting me! A bug. A beetle. Get it off. Get it off!"

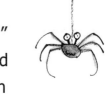

"Calm down, my little friend," said Bart. "It's only a spider. There – on the back of your neck. Got it!"

And Bart plucked it off me and held it, dangling, in front of his own face.

"KILL IT! KILL IT!" I cried.

"No!" said Bart protectively. "It's lovely!"

"And possibly poisonous," observed Tommo. "I'm with Pip on this one."

"I am not going to kill it," Bart insisted. "I think spiders are amazing. Eight little legs. A headful of eyeballs. And all that incredible web-making equipment. I love 'em!"

Then he set the spider on his forehead, and it crawled away into his hair.

I cringed. "THAT'S DISGUSTING!"

"And potentially life-threatening!" added Tommo.

"**Nonsense**," Bart shrugged. "I have never been bitten by a spider in my **Life**. Or any other bug, for that matter."

"There's a first time for everything," said Tommo.

"Not for me," said Bart. "I love those little creatures, and they know it. That's why they leave me alone."

"Yeah, they're too busy burrowing into your scalp," I winced.

"That is not a burrowing spider," Bart explained, "so there is nothing to worry about. I know because, as you may have observed, I am a keen student of all things buggy!"

"You certainly know how to 'bug' us!" Tommo grunted.

"Laugh all you like," Bart answered. "Anyone who knows me will tell you. Bugs are my speciality. Ask my aunt Gomer."

"How many aunts do you have, exactly?" I asked.

"Plenty," Bart noted. "But my extensive family is not the point. During the summers I would spend weeks at a time with my aunt Gomer. She was a small, wiry woman with hair like a hedgehog. Disturbing, but she had a lovely disposition. My uncle Hosea adored her. He had this curious pet name for her. A strange, nonsense word he used: '**My Little Tiggywinkle**'. It was she who fostered my passion for insects. She would point them out to me as we walked together or foraged for nuts in the undergrowth."

"You foraged for nuts?" asked Tommo.

"It was a hard time," Bart remembered. "And she liked nuts. And grubs. Anyway, she would show me the different insects and then send me out to collect them. And I would always return, the sun setting at the end of the day, with bugs in my hand or on my head or any place I could store them. I remember one time in particular . . .

"'Barty,' she said to me, 'settle down and **STOP** your jumping about. You act like you have **ants** in your **pants**!' And I did."

Just then, Jesus made an announcement. "I'm going up the mountain," he said, "and I need three of you to come with me. Peter, James and John, how about you?"

"There they go again," Bart sighed. "If only I had put my hand up and answered Jesus' question, that could have been us."

"Go on, Tommo," I said. "Say it. I know you want to."

"Nah," Tommo grunted. "If they want to go traipsing up a mountain while the rest of us relax, that's their business. Flippin' fishermen."

"**Ooh, look!**" Bart interrupted. "Did you see that?"

"See what, Big Fella?" I shrugged.

"THAT BUTTERFLY!" Bart exclaimed. "It just fluttered by my head. It was amazing!"

"Sorry," I said. "Missed it. Had my eyes shut."

"Me too," added Tommo, yawning. "But we'll take your word for it. It was a butterfly. It was amazing. Now for that little nap."

"But you don't understand!" Bart continued. "That was no ordinary amazing butterfly. That was a DEAD MAN'S BOTTOM!"

"Dead Man's Bottom?" I asked.

"So called because the markings on its wings bear a striking resemblance to a sailor who has fallen out of his boat and is left floating, bottom up, in the middle of the Dead Sea!"

"Now that's a pretty picture," grunted Tommo.

"Do sailors even sail boats on the Dead Sea?" I wondered.

"And aren't we miles away from there, anyway?" added Tommo.

"EXACTLY!" Bart cried. "That's what makes this so special! And that's why we have to follow it!"

"To catch it?" I suggested.

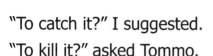

"To kill it?" asked Tommo.

"No!" Bart cried. "To give it a little pat on the head! It's lovely! Anything else would be cruel."

"If I was a butterfly," said Tommo, "I wouldn't want you patting me on the head."

"If I was a butterfly," I said. "I wouldn't want you anywhere near me."

"If I was a butterfly," said Bart, looking wistfully at the sky, "I'd thank the Lord for giving me wings." And then he added, "C'MON, if we hurry we can still find it."

"I think I'll just hang out here for a while," I yawned.

"Yeah, knock yourself out, Big Fella," yawned Tommo too. "Let us know how it all turns out."

"But I need your **help**," Bart pleaded.

"I'm not going," I said.

"Not even if the spider that is on my head decides to find a new home?" Bart suggested, running his fingers through his hair and pulling out the squiggling creature.

"There you go, little fella. Seems that my buddy Pip would like you to visit him for a while."

I cringed. "Keep that thing **away** from me, Bart! I'm warning you . . ."

Bart held the spider to his ear.

"But he says he's lonely. He wants a new home. On Pip Street!"

"THAT IS NOT FUNNY!" I cried.

"What's that, Mr Spider?" Bart went on. "You say you can't move to Pip Street if Pip Street moves up the mountain? I see!"

"All right, I'm coming. I'm coming," I moaned, struggling to my feet.

"Now he wants to go to Tommo Lane!" Bart grinned.

"**yeah, yeah, yeah**," moaned Tommo. "I get the picture. And as I'm not getting any sleep anyway . . ."

"That's the spirit!" Bart grinned again.
Then he dropped the spider back onto his head
and said, "Back on top of
Bart Manor, my little friend."
And the three of us
set off after the
butterfly.

We climbed for ten minutes, then fifteen. The mountainside was steep.

"This is a waste of time," Tommo complained. "There are no amazing butterflies here. Or anything else amazing to look at, for that matter. Just rocks and dirt and scraggly, brown shrubs."

"LET'S GO BACK, BART!" I pleaded. "We're never going to find that butterfly again. It was a fluke."

But Bart would not be persuaded. "We will see that Dead Man's Bottom again," he assured us. "I promise. And what a special moment that will be!"

And then I stopped. And gasped. "LOOK! There's your butterfly – in that clump of bushes!"

Bart was ecstatic! "Dead Man's Bottom. **Dead Man's Bottom!**" he cried. And he launched his oversized self in the general direction of the shrubbery.

Tommo and I wandered away, desperate for a little rest.

"That oughta keep him busy for a while," Tommo whispered.

"Let's hope so," I said. And then I gasped again.

"Not another flippin' butterfly?" moaned Tommo.

"No," I whispered. "Worse. Look over there. It's Jesus and the guys."

"So?" Tommo shrugged.

"So, we're not supposed to be here," I reminded him. "He specifically asked for just the three of them to go with him."

"Well, we can't hear anything from over here. So if it's some kind of secret, we're fine."

"But we can see. And if you can see what I can see, then I think maybe we're not supposed to be . . . seeing it!"

Strange as it may seem, Jesus had started to . . . "GLOW," I said aloud. "I think that's the word I would use for it."

"I concur," Tommo nodded. "He is definitely . . . glowing. Though how or why I do not know."

"Perhaps it would be best if we hid ourselves behind that small tree over there," I suggested.

"Again, I concur," Tommo said. "But what about Bart?"

"Well, he's looking the other way," I answered. "And he's so busy trying to find that butterfly that I don't think he's actually noticed."

"**Thanks for the light, guys!**" Bart called back, his head still buried in the bushes. "I can see loads better!"

"**Correction**," I said, "perhaps he's noticed just a bit."

Meanwhile, Jesus glowed brighter and brighter. And when he was so bright that Tommo and I could hardly stand to look at him, he was joined by two other shining figures.

Hands in front of our faces, eyes squinting just to see, Tommo and I tried to figure out who they were.

"ANgels?" I wondered out loud.

"Could be," Tommo nodded. "But the one on the far side looks like he's carrying something."

"STONE TABLETS!" I cried. "The Ten Commandments! It's Moses!"

"But he died thousands of years ago," gasped Tommo.

"After he led our people out of slavery," I nodded. "Amazing. And you know what? I think I've figured out who the other fella is as well. Do you see the fiery chariot behind him?"

"OF COURSE!" said Tommo. "It's the prophet Elijah! Maybe the greatest prophet our people ever had."

"So if these guys lived all those years ago," I asked, "what do you suppose they're doing here, with Jesus, now?"

"Dunno," Tommo shrugged. "Maybe God is trying to show us – well, that lot, strictly speaking – that Jesus is special like Moses and Elijah. And speaking of that lot – what's Peter doing?"

"He's waving his arms about. It looks like he's making the shape of a tent with his hands. Wish he'd speak up."

"Flippin' fisherman," Tommo grunted, straining to hear. "Wait. You're right. He wants to build tents. One for each of them. So he can stay here and talk with them, I guess."

"Fair enough," I said. "Those are three amazing individuals!"

Just then a cloud came down from the sky and surrounded them all. And a voice came out from the cloud. A voice so loud that no one could fail to hear it.

"This is my son," the voice said. "LISTEN TO HIM!"

And when the cloud lifted, Moses and Elijah were gone, and Jesus was standing there, all alone.

"Guess one is more special than the rest, though," Tommo concluded.

"Looks that way," I agreed. "So was that a vision – or did it really happen?"

"Don't know," said Tommo, "but we'd better get out of here. And we'd better find Bart."

And so we did. And when we did, he was holding a butterfly in his hand.

"Dead Man's Bottom!" he grinned. "And just look at the expression on your faces. I knew you'd be amazed!"

I looked at Tommo. Tommo looked at me.

Bart would never have believed us anyway, so without saying another word, we marched our big friend back down the mountainside.

When we reached the bottom, Jesus was there, waiting.

"So where have you three been?" he asked. "Ummm, up the mountainside, Jesus," I muttered.

"That's it," nodded Tommo.

Jesus looked a little concerned. A little worried. And maybe just a little annoyed.

"But I specifically asked just Peter and James and John to go with me." And then he added, "You didn't see anything, did you?"

And before Tommo or I could explain, Bart shouted, "We did, Jesus! And it was amazing!"

"I see," Jesus nodded, looking more anxious still . . . "And what exactly did you see?"

"You'll never believe it, Jesus," Bart beamed.

"Try me," said Jesus.

"IT'S SPECTACULAR!" Bart added.

"I'll be the judge of that," Jesus said.

"It's the most unbelievable thing ever!" Bart exclaimed.

"So tell me," said Jesus. "What was it?"
And Bart held out his hand and said,
"A Dead Man's Bottom!"

There was a long and
uncomfortable pause. And
then finally Tommo muttered, "It's a butterfly,
Jesus."

"Quite rare apparently," I mumbled. And Jesus
grinned. Then he chuckled. Then he laughed
out loud and clapped us on our shoulders.

"You're ABSOLUTELY right!" he agreed.
"That's an amazing butterfly, lads!"

And when he had walked away, still smiling,
Tommo and I breathed a relieved sigh and Bart
began to itch.

"**What's up**, Big Fella?" I asked.

"Lost your butterfly?" asked Tommo.

"NO," he said. "It's that spider. The one that was living on my head in Bart Manor. He appears to have moved to the basement."

And he shook his head. And his legs. And his Big Bart bottom.